W9-BUQ-097

BEAR-OLOGY™

Fascinating Bear Facts, Tales & Trivia

SYLVIA DOLSON

PIXYJACK PRESS LLC

BEAR-OLOGY: FASCINATING BEAR FACTS, TALES & TRIVIA

Copyright © 2009 by Sylvia Dolson

No part of this book may be reproduced, stored in a retrieval system or transmitted in any form, or by any means, electronic, mechanical, photocopying, recording or otherwise, without prior written permission of the publisher, except by a reviewer, who may quote brief passages in review.

Published by PixyJack Press, LLC   PO Box 149, Masonville, CO 80541 USA

First Edition 2009

9 8 7 6 5 4 3 2 1

ISBN 978-0-9773724-5-4

Library of Congress Cataloging-in-Publication Data
    Dolson, Sylvia.
      Bear-ology : fascinating bear facts, tales & trivia / Sylvia Dolson. – 1st ed.
      p. cm.
      Includes bibliographical references.
      Summary: "An informative review of the world's bears (including black bears, grizzlies, polar bears and giant pandas) reveals bear behavior and biology, past and present mythologies, plus modern day perceptions and human-bear coexisting issues; complete with numerous photos, illustrations and trivia"–Provided by publisher.
      ISBN 978-0-9773724-5-4
      1. Bears–Miscellanea. I. Title.
      QL737.C27D64 2009
      599.78–dc22   2008053831

Printed in Canada on chlorine-free, 100% postconsumer recycled paper.

ENVIRONMENTAL BENEFITS: PixyJack Press saved the following resources by printing this book on chlorine-free paper made with 100% post-consumer waste: 35 fully grown trees, 25 million BTUs of energy, 3,093 pounds of greenhouse gases, 12,837 gallons of water, and 1,648 pounds of solid waste.

Front cover photos by Sylvia Dolson. Back cover photo by Irene Sheppard.

Illustrations by Evelyn Kirkaldy.

Book design by LaVonne Ewing.

For Jeanie —
the bear who inspires me every day
to make the world a better place
for both bears and people

REVIEWS

"*Bear-ology* is an entertaining and informative review of bear behaviour, biology and mythology filled with tantalizing tidbits of ursid trivia. Dolson's style is easy and relaxed without sacrificing content or accuracy."

– Dr. Wayne Lynch, celebrated natural history writer and wildlife photographer

"Who'd imagine it could be this much fun learning so much valuable information about bears? There's absolutely nothing 'bear-related' missing from *Bear-ology*. Read it and be amazed."

– Ann Bryant, Executive Director of The BEAR League

"*Bear-ology* is very entertaining, educational, and an important reference source for biologists and the general public with an interest in separating facts from common myths about the lives of bears."

– Dr. John J. Beecham, Wildlife Consultant for Human-Bear Conflicts / Orphan Bear Rehabilitation

"Through hundreds of smiles and reflections, *Bear-ology* will open a door and invite you into the fascinating world of bears and people who care about them."

– Dr. Stephen Herrero, author of *Bear Attacks: Their Causes and Avoidance*, Past President of IBA

"One of the best all-you-want-to-know-about-bears books ever written. Sylvia has done a remarkable job in relaying in simple language blended with wonderful photos and illustrations the fascinating ecology, behaviour, lore and history of bears that can only help us achieve a better coexistence with these wild and sentient beings that so symbolize the wilderness."

– Wayne McCrory, Bear Biologist, British Columbia, Canada

"*Bear-ology* is smart, informative, entertaining, accessible and a must-read for bear fans everywhere."

– Benjamin Kilham, author of *Among the Bears: Raising Orphan Cubs in the Wild*

contents

continued

Real & Not-So-Real Famous Bears

PREFACE — The Lives of Bears

I am partway up Bear Paw, one of the many ski runs on the north face of Whistler Mountain, when I spot the familiar chocolate hue of Jeanie's fur in a small island of trees. She lies in the cool shade of the firs on this late May evening. The ground is damp from a recent rain and the air is heavy with the scent of pine. It is dusk; there is just enough light to make out the distinct cream patch on her chest.

I know it is Jeanie in an instant, for we have met on this mountain many times before, but this is the first time this year. She is only recently out of her winter den, and I'm excited to see whether she has cubs with her. A branch cracks behind her, and then another. And then a cinnamon cub tumbles Winnie the Pooh-like out of the tree above her head, landing on her back with a squeal. She gently shoves him to the side, only to watch him rear up on his hind legs and leap at her head. He wants to wrestle, and she is happy to oblige.

Over the years, I have spent time in the company of many bears, from the black bears of Whistler to the great browns of Alaska and the winter-white polar bears of Churchill. Jeanie, however, holds a very special place in my heart. She is about 20 years old now and resides with me and 10,000 other human beings in and around Whistler, a four-season resort community nestled in the coastal mountains of British Columbia, Canada. The center of Whistler is the Whistler-Blackcomb Ski Resort, one of the world's premier downhill skiing destinations and the official alpine skiing venue for the 2010 Winter Olympic Games. The town proper is spread out across and down the valley, a dozen distinct neighborhoods joined by roads and wide ribbons of forest.

Whistler's urban landscape was specifically designed to accommodate the natural environment. The idea was to design the town in a way that allowed it to blend in with the surrounding forest rather than dominate it. While the goal was laudable, it also created some problems, for this is prime bear habitat. It essentially created a situation in which bears and people were forced to coexist side-by-side throughout the entire community.

Jeanie has been the matriarch of Whistler Mountain since I moved to Whistler in 1996. She has become an icon in our community and a symbol of our attempts to learn how to coexist with bears. Residents follow her life story in the newspaper, and teachers often use Jeanie's story to teach children about bears everywhere. Like Olympic gold medal winner Ross Rebagliati, who also calls Whistler home, she has become something of a local celebrity.

But her life has not been easy. When natural foods run out in the late fall, she sometimes finds herself rummaging through garbage in the middle of Whistler Village. She has been trapped and moved out of busy urban areas and sent back onto the mountain. Biologists have fitted a radio collar around her neck and tracked her movements. Police have fired rubber bullets and bear bangers at her to teach her to stay away from people. She has raised five sets of cubs since I have known her, not one of which has survived long enough to raise cubs of its own. Jake, the little cub that wanted so badly to play wrestle with his mother, was killed by officials when he was three years old for routinely raiding unsecured garbage cans in search of food.

It is for Jeanie and Jake and wild bears everywhere that I have compiled this book. My experiences with Jeanie and dozens of other bears have allowed me to look through a small window into the lives of bears. This book will help to promote a deeper understanding of these intelligent and vulnerable animals, one that transcends the unfounded fears based on years of misinformation, sensationalized media stories, and exaggerated campfire tales. I hope people who read this book, many of whom may never have had the opportunity of living or recreating in bear country, will gain even the smallest semblance of the true nature and essence of the bear—one of the most amazing animals on planet earth.

— *Sylvia Dolson, the Bear Lady of Whistler*

Dispelling Myths

Bears have fascinated us for centuries. As one of the most adaptable and versatile mammals on earth, their behavior stirs fear, awe, wonder, and curiosity in us. Unfortunately, there are many myths surrounding the lives and behavior of bears which impact negatively on people's imaginations.

Stories of ferocious attacks by blood-thirsty bears on defenseless hikers make great lead stories in the media. The overwhelming sense conveyed in these stories is that bears are dangerous, mean creatures who are an extreme threat to people in any circumstance. Of course this is inaccurate at best and unhelpful at worst.

Another commonly found myth is that bears are cuddly creatures that resemble the teddy bears we owned as kids. While there is no doubt that bears hold the fascination to trigger children's imaginations, it is important that the stories we share with our children be based on fact and not fiction.

It is important to dispel both myths—the myth based on fear, and the one based on a misplaced belief that bears are tame, cuddly animals. Bears are intelligent and resourceful wild mammals that deserve our respect.

A greater knowledge of the behavior, ecology, and habitat needs of bears is crucial if we are to learn to coexist peacefully with this magnificent megafauna. *[www.americanbear.org]*

Myth #1: Bears have poor eyesight.

FACT: Bears see in color and have good vision, similar to humans. Their night vision is excellent *(see page 28)* and they are particularly attuned to detecting movement.

Myth #2: If a bear is standing on its hind legs, it's about to charge.

FACT: Actually, the bear is just trying to better identify what has caught its attention. It is easier for a bear to see, hear, and smell things from a standing position, than down on all fours.

Myth #3: If a bear charges you, climb a tree.

FACT: Despite all their timidness on the ground, black bears seem to feel more courageous in trees. Bears sometimes kill each other by throwing their opponents out of trees. The bear below has the advantage because the bear above cannot easily hang on and face downward to fight back. Also, the lower bear seems confident of these advantages and some bears have even come up trees after people who thought climbing was prudent. Grizzlies, too, can climb—perhaps not as quickly, but they have been known to attack people who climbed trees to escape.

Myth #4: Bear bells are the best way to avoid a surprise encounter.

FACT: Bear bells have no biological significance to a bear, so they don't relate the sound of bells to people approaching. The best way to alert bears to your presence is by talking loudly, singing songs or breaking sticks. Try to hike in a group on established trails during daylight hours.

Myth #5: One of the most dangerous encounters is getting between a mother black bear and her cubs.

FACT: Because black bears can tree their cubs, it is rare for them to attack a person in defense of cubs. However, if you are anywhere near a mother grizzly's cubs, she might very well perceive you as a threat. Chances are she may just bluff charge and stop short of an attack. You need to do whatever you can to show her that you are not a threat, otherwise the consequences could be tragic. Be quiet, make yourself smaller and retreat.

Bears are actually attracted to pepper spray residue if it is sprayed on the ground or on objects. Never spray it around a tent or on yourself. When used defensively, pepper spray must be sprayed directly in the attacking bear's eyes or nose.

Myth #6: Carrying a rifle is safer than pepper spray.

FACT: A person's chance of incurring serious injury from a charging grizzly doubles when bullets are fired versus when pepper spray is used. *[Dr. Stephen Herrero]* Those injured defending themselves with pepper spray vs. firearms experienced shorter duration attacks and less severe injuries. *[U.S. Fish and Wildlife Service]*

Myth #7: Bears are unpredictable.

FACT: Bears are no more unpredictable than any other animal, including humans. Bears use body language and vocalizations to show their intentions. Learning about their behavior can be beneficial to people who live or recreate in bear country *(see pages 78 – 83)*.

Myth #8: Once a bear has tasted human food, it won't eat wild food any more.

FACT: Bears naturally prefer wild food unless it is difficult to find and human food is too easy to get. Even the worst food-conditioned bears still eat natural food whenever it is plentiful. Human-bear conflicts usually increase when natural foods run out—a good time for people to be more vigilant of bear attractants on their property; such as bird feed, dog food, fruit trees/berry bushes, barbecue grease and compost.

Myth #9: Shooting or relocating a 'nuisance' bear will solve the problem.

FACT: Removing the bear and not the attractant will only create a newly available habitat niche so another bear can move right back in, creating a vicious cycle of conflict and killing.

Myth #10: Bears that wander into inhabited areas such as campsites, communities or cottage country are "problem" bears.

FACT: Bears may travel hundreds of miles in search of food and sometimes pass through human-use areas while making their daily excursions. If you have stored your food and garbage properly, the bear will likely move on. Remember, so-called "problem" bears are not born, they're created through human carelessness and neglect. If bears are hanging around, something is attracting them. Removing the attraction will usually solve the problem.

Myth #11: Bears can't run down hill.

FACT: Bears can run up hills, down hills or sideways—and they can do it at more than 60 kilometers an hour (37 mph). A brown bear in Denali National Park in Alaska was clocked at 66 kph (41 mph)!

Myth #12: People traveling in bear country are often attacked.

FACT: Bear attacks are extremely rare. Although there are thousands of human-bear encounters every year, only a very few result in personal injury. Most bears will actually retreat before you are even aware of their presence. It is still important, however, to stay alert and know the bear-safe facts.

Myth #13: It is dangerous to go into bear country when menstruating.

FACT: Current evidence suggests that menstruation does not increase the likelihood of an attack by a black or grizzly bear, but tampons are recommended over pads. They may be disposed of by burning and then packing out the remains.

Myth #14: Bears are carnivores.

FACT: Although classified in the order Carnivora, grizzly and black bears are omnivores, meaning that they eat both plants and animals. Only 10 to 15 percent of their diets consist of meat, which includes fish, insects, and other mammals, like squirrels.

Myth #15: Play dead during an attack.

FACT: Playing dead will work if you're being attacked by a mother grizzly defending her cubs. But it is the wrong thing to do if you're being attacked by a predatory bear. If a bear attacks (particularly a black bear) in an offensive manner and physical contact is made, fight

for your life. Kick, punch, hit the bear with rocks or sticks or any improvised weapon you can find. A predatory bear usually stalks its prey and attacks from behind. It is often silent and the bear does not exhibit any defensive behaviors like huffing or slapping the ground. Its ears may be laid back and its head held low, with its intent focused directly on you.

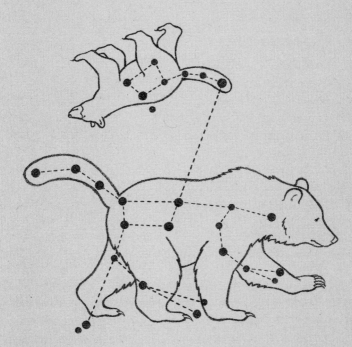

Bears in the Night Sky

Ursa Major (which is Latin for *great bear*) is perhaps one of the most recognizable patterns of stars in the night sky. As kids, we came to know this group of seven stars as the Big Dipper. The handle of the Dipper is thought to be the great bear's tail and the dipper's cup is the bear's flank.

This constellation has a lot of history behind it. Stories about Ursa Major date back to the Ice Age. The myths are so common and widespread in both the Old and New World that they are thought to have been carried across the Bering Land Bridge during the migrations from Siberia to Alaska—about 25,000 years ago. It is even thought possible that the constellation actually got its name 50,000 years ago when a Paleolithic bear cult existed. It's

The Little Dipper

Ursa Minor is Latin for little bear. This constellation vaguely resembles a baby bear with an unusually long tail. The tail was said to have been lengthened from that usually expected for a bear, due to it being held by the tail and spun around the pole.

also one of the few star groups mentioned in the Bible (Job 9:9; 38:32).

Interestingly, although the pattern represents a variety of objects to many cultures—a plow, wagon, coffin, skunk, camel, shark, canoe, bushel, sickle, even a hog's jaw—several different cultures saw a big bear in the sky. Native American mythology tells of three hunters pursuing the great bear. While a Roman myth depicts both bears, Ursa Major and Ursa Minor (Little Dipper) in a story of love, jealousy and revenge. The ancient Greeks had a few different stories to explain how the animal ended up there. One story tells of Zeus and one of his many infidelities. Zeus was married to Hera, but fell in love with Callisto. When Hera learned of the affair she swore vengeance, so Zeus turned Callisto into a bear to disguise her from his furious wife. Looking like a bear, however, carried its own risks. One day Callisto's son, Arcas, saw a bear—really his mother—and raised his spear to kill it. To protect Callisto, Zeus quickly changed Arcas into a bear cub. Then, to head off future disasters, he put both bears among the stars. Hera saw this and finally got her revenge. She decreed that both bears would never rest again and doomed them to rotate endlessly in the night sky. ～

trivial but true

Keeping Time Before Clocks The main timekeeper in the sky is Ursa Major, the Great Bear, which rotates about the north celestial pole each night and through the year, making it a clock and a calendar.

Running on All Fours

Bears can lumber along on all fours, or stand up on their hind feet and gesture with their front paws. Ursa Major, in its travels throughout the heavens, constantly changes from quadrupedal to bipedal positions, seeming to run along on all fours nearest the horizon and then rising to its hind feet to begin the ascent back into the sky.

A little yearling black bear seems to have found his way into someone's backyard. He's not lost; he is looking for food scraps. *PHOTO: CHRIS BENGE*

did you know?

Finding Your Way The magnetic compass was developed 2,000 years ago as an aid to finding the best aspect for new buildings, and it was immediately adapted as a navigational aid. In the original compass, the pointer was shaped like the Ursa Minor constellation, since the star at the end of the Little Dipper's handle is Polaris, the North Star, or north celestial pole.

Get the Bear Facts

How Many Bears Are There?

It's hard to count bears. No adequate census exists on which to base worldwide population estimates of bears. Scientists provide estimates based on various estimating models, but many of these guesstimates are considered unreliable—particularly those from Third World countries.

Nonetheless, according to recent assessments by the World Conservation Union (IUCN) Bear and Polar Bear Specialist Groups, six out of the world's eight species of bears are threatened with extinction. Asia and South America are revealed as the areas most in need of urgent conservation action.

Only the **American black bear** is secure throughout its range, which encompasses Canada, the United States, and Mexico. At 900,000 strong, there are more than twice as many American black bears than all the other species of bears combined.

The total world population of **brown bears** is estimated to exceed 200,000. Russia has the largest number

number of brown bears, believed to be greater than 100,000, while estimates in the U.S. are around 33,000, Canada 25,000, and Europe 14,000. Brown bears, the most wide-spread bear, are not listed as threatened globally because large numbers still inhabit Russia, Canada, Alaska, and some parts of Europe. Nevertheless, very small, isolated and highly vulnerable populations exist in southern Europe and cen-

tral and southern Asia. Several brown bear populations in North America are protected under national or provincial/state laws. Grizzly bears—brown bears living in the interior—are considered Threatened or Endangered under the U.S. Endangered Species Act in many parts of the lower forty-eight states, including northwest Montana, northern Idaho, and north-central Washington. Despite much opposition, the grizzly was delisted in the Greater Yellowstone area in 2007. In Canada, the grizzly bear is listed as a Species of Special Concern at the federal level. A small subpopulation in south-central British Columbia is listed as Threatened and is undergoing recovery efforts.

There are about 20,000–25,000 **polar bears** in the circumpolar

trivial but true

How many teeth does a polar bear have? 42

trivial but true

A'hoy matey The polar bear is classified as a marine mammal. Its feet are partially webbed for swimming, and its fur is water-repellent. Polar bears have been known to swim more than 100 kilometers (60 miles) without a rest. The polar bear's entire body is covered in fur, even the bottom of its paws—helping it to withstand the cold arctic waters. Even their nostrils close to prevent water from getting in.

Arctic. They live throughout the ice-covered waters in northern Canada, Greenland, Norway's Svalbard archipeligo, the Russian Federation, and Alaska, United States; their range being limited by the southern extent of sea ice. Two-thirds of the world's polar bears could be threatened with extinction by 2050 due to melting sea ice resulting from global warming.

Sloth bears are found only on the Indian subcontinent, with a sub-species living in Sri Lanka. Once found in many forested areas across India, these bears are now found only in a few scattered habitats. They have found sanctuary mainly in reserves set up to protect tigers. The current population is estimated to be around 4,000 and is steadily declining.

trivial but true

Which bear has the longest tail? The sloth bear has the longest tail in the bear family. It is 15–18 cm (6–7 inches) long. The giant panda has the second longest tail, 10–15 cm (4–6 inches) long.

The **giant panda** remains in the Endangered category on the IUCN Red List of Threatened Species. There are only about 1,600 giant pandas left in the wild. That status remains unchanged despite enormous efforts in China directed towards their conservation, including the establishment of nearly sixty panda reserves, a ban on logging, and widespread reforestation programs. They are found only in a few mountain ranges in central and western China, mainly in Sichuan, Shaanxi, and Gansu provinces.

did you know?

A life of leisure? Giant pandas certainly seem to enjoy a life of leisure, but how many hours a day do these gentle giants actually sleep? A) 4 hours; B) 6 hours; or C) 10 hours

Answer: Four hours. Giant pandas live almost exclusively on bamboo, but, unfortunately, bamboo isn't that nutritious. So pandas must spend as much time as they can tearing down and eating bamboo thickets, leaving little time for napping.

The **spectacled bear** dwells in low-level tropical forests and alpine meadows along the Andean slopes in Venezuela, Columbia, Ecuador, Peru, and Bolivia. Small populations can be found in southern Panama and northern Argentina. Population data are sketchy, but some estimates suggest fewer than 3,000 spectacled bears may remain in the wild today. Their population is listed as Vulnerable and is decreasing.

A spectacled bear's face, neck and chest markings are like human fingerprints, unique to each bear.

did you know?

Can you name all the bear species in South America? That's easy! There is only one. The spectacled bear, also called the Andean bear, is the only bear species found on the entire South American continent. It is called a spectacled bear because some members of this species have white rings of fur around their eyes which look like spectacles (eyeglasses).

Where does the spectacled bear find its favorite food? A) underground; B) on the ground; C) high in the trees; or D) wherever it can find it.

Answer: C. The spectacled bear's favorite food is the spiny leaves of the bromeliad, which grows in the tops of some trees.

The world's smallest species of bear, the **sun bear**, whose population size is unknown, has been classed as Vulnerable. Sun bears live in mainland Southeast Asia as far west as the eastern edge of India, as far north as Yunnan Province in China, and south and east to Sumatra and Borneo, respectively.

Asiatic black bears are classed as Vulnerable with a guesstimated population of 36,000–76,000. They are found over a wide area of southern Asia along the mountains from Afghanistan, through Pakistan and northern India, Nepal, Sikkim, Bhutan, into Burma and northeastern China. They are also found in southeastern Russia, Taiwan, and on the Japanese islands of Honshu and Shikoku.

trivial but true

Moon Bear The Asiatic black bear's scientific name *(Selenarctos thibetanus)* literally means "moon bear of Tibet." It is called the moon bear because of the large yellowish cresent-shaped marking on its chest.

How Long Do Bears Live?

Bears can live well into their 20s or even 30s in the wild. Some bears in captivity have even lived past 40. Debby, the oldest known polar bear, died in November 2008 at the Assiniboine Park Zoo (Winnipeg, Canada) where she had lived since 1967 after being captured as a orphaned cub in the Russian Arctic in 1966.

Bears' chances of reaching that age are pretty slim though. The survival rate of cubs is generally less than 50 percent. Adult bears have an annual survival rate of 50 to 80 percent, depending on the location. They generally have good health and do not get sick. Humans cause most of their deaths.

Bears that live in heavily hunted areas rarely ever see their tenth birthday and often only live to be four or five years old.

How Fast Do Bears Run?

Bears can run more than 60 kilometers an hour (37 mph)—that's more than twice as fast as an Olympic sprinter. In fact, a bear can outrun a race horse over short distances, but has little endurance. To put their speed in perspective, bears can run 15 meters per second (50 feet per second).

A young grizzly rips across Knight Inlet in British Columbia to avoid conflict with a more dominant male. *PHOTO: SYLVIA DOLSON*

How Well Do Bears Smell, See and Hear?

Bears live in a rich and complex scent-defined world. They navigate the world with their noses, unlike people for whom sight is the predominant sense and smell is probably one of the least used senses. Bears constantly gather, process, and exchange information using their sense of smell. It helps them find food and mates, identify cubs, and avoid danger. Like most large-muzzled carnivores, their smelling ability is extremely sensitive, with one hundred times more nasal mucosa area than a human. A bear can detect smells from miles and miles away. A complex system of social messages are communicated through trails of airborne scent; scent transferred to twigs, branches, and grasses; and scents left on purpose by tree rubbing or biting, as well as scat or urine

marks. In the ursine world, these messages form the daily newspaper.

A bear's hearing ability is excellent, and like dogs, bears hear high pitches, exceeding human frequency range and sensitivity.

One common misconception is that bears have poor eyesight, but evidence indicates that bears' eyesight is comparable to ours. Bears see in color and have good close-up vision. They can see well at night and in the daytime.

A bear's sense of smell is about seven times better than a bloodhound's or 2,100 times better than a human's.
PHOTO: SYLVIA DOLSON

Why are bears eyes set close together? Most predator's eyes are set close together to allow for binocular vision (the field of vision of both eyes intersects to provide more accurate depth perception). While many bears are not really predatory, they are of the order Carnivora and in their earlier evolution, relied much more on a meat diet. Usually the eyes of prey are set farther apart to allow for better peripheral vision, enabling them to detect danger from a wider field of vision.

PHOTO: SYLVIA DOLSON

Using their keen sense of smell, grizzly bears can detect clams buried in the sand. It's not uncommon to see grizzlies meandering across the tidal flats, nose to the ground. A successful mollusk-hunting bear will use their claws to pull a clam apart and then extract the meat with their lips and tongue.

trivial but true

Green-Eye? If you've ever photographed a bear with a flash, you would notice that the eyes appear oddly large and green. Like many animals, bears' eyes have a reflective layer called the tapetum lucidum lining the back of the eyeball. This layer reflects light back through the retina, allowing light to stimulate light-sensitive cells in the retina a second time, thereby improving night vision. This is what gives dogs, cats and many nocturnal animals that distinct, bright eyeshine when they are flashed with a light at night.

Bears Have Great Memories

Bears remember what they have learned, especially with respect to the locations of food sources. As a result, bears readily form associations between the presence of people or developed areas and the likelihood that food will also be available. When natural foods are scarce, bears are likely to become highly adept at accessing human food and garbage, even if it means going through the kitchen window to investigate the contents of the refrigerator. Bears seem to be able to outsmart us at every turn. With time, opportunity and motivation, they

 learn how to turn door knobs and even penetrate so-called bear-proof waste containers. From an ursine perspective, where there's a will, there's a way.

PHOTO: IRENE SHEPPARD

How Smart Are Bears?

With intelligence comparable to that of the great apes,
bears are highly evolved social
animals—they show insight,
planning, and intentional
communication. Bears often
share friendship, resources,
and security. They form hier-
archies and have structured

kinship relationships. They're all individuals with unique person-
alities. *[Ben Kilham]*

Of all the carnivores, bears have the highest brain-to-body
mass ratio. In fact, as the most intelligent animals in North America,
bears can generalize at the simple concept level. According to Dr.
Lynn Rogers, an example of this type of learning (or ability to generalize) might be a bear who smells formic acid from ant colonies
(a favorite food) and then later bites into insulation made with
formaldehyde that gives off formic acid as it breaks down, such
as the insulation found in hot tub covers, snowmobile seat covers,
refrigerators. Bears have even been known to use tools to assist in
carrying out tasks. They have an extraordinary capacity to learn
and excellent long-term memories.

Although scientists don't know how they do it, bears have
amazing navigational abilities, far superior to humans, and are able
to travel widely without becoming lost. Because they travel such
long distances and through a variety of habitats to find food, learning and remembering is very valuable to bears. *[Dr. Lynn Rogers]*

Brown Bear, Grizzly, or Kodiak?

Brown bears are one of the eight species of bears, in the family
Ursidae. Their scientific name is *Ursus arctos*. Grizzly and Kodiak
are common names.

The range of the brown bear is the widest of any species of

bear in the world. They are found in parts of Europe, Asia, Russia, and Japan. In North America, brown bears live in western Canada, and in the states of Alaska, Wyoming, Montana, Idaho, and Washington— where they are

A female grizzly rests in the sea grass at Hallo Bay, Alaska. *PHOTO: SYLVIA DOLSON*

commonly referred to as grizzlies, originally named after their silver-tipped guard hairs or grizzled appearance. Kodiaks are the bigger bears of the coast and live mainly on Kodiak Island as well as on some smaller surrounding islands in Alaska.

Matters of Size...How Big Is a Bear?

Brown Bears (Grizzlies) There is considerable variability in the size of brown bears from different areas, depending on the quality of food available. Seasonal considerations also need to be taken into account—for instance, some bears can weigh almost twice as much in the fall as they might weigh in spring, especially pregnant females. Adult males may weigh 135 to 390 kilograms (300 to 860 pounds) compared with 95 to 205 kg (205 to 455 lbs) for females. At birth, cubs weigh 340 to 680 grams (11 to 22 oz). That means grizzly bear mommas outweigh their cubs by about 300 times.

The largest bears are found on the west coast of British Columbia and Alaska, and on islands along coastal Alaska, such as Kodiak and Admiralty. There, males average over 300 kg (660 lbs) and females over 200 kg (440 lbs). Brown bears from the interior ranges of North America, Europe, and the sub-Arctic are roughly two-thirds the size of their Alaskan or Kamchatkan cousins. The largest brown bear ever measured was a Kodiak bear who weighed over 1,134 kg (2,500 lbs) and was almost 14 feet tall when standing—that's bigger than the biggest known polar bear.

Black Bears Black bears vary considerably in size, again depending on food availability and the season. Adult male black bears typically weigh 60 to 300 kg (130 to 660 lbs); females are smaller and weigh 40 to 140 kg (90 to 308 lbs). At birth, cubs weigh 225 to 330 grams (7 to 11 oz). Standing up on its hind feet, a black bear can be up to seven feet tall. The largest black bear on record, weighing 400 kg (880 lbs), was hunted in North Carolina in 1999.

This adult male black bear weighs about 180 kg (400 lbs). *PHOTO: SYLVIA DOLSON*

Polar Bears The polar bear is the largest land carnivore alive in the world today. Adult males weigh from 400 to 600 kg (880 to 1,320 lbs) and occasionally exceed 800 kg (1,760 lbs). Females are about half the size of males and normally weigh 200 to 300 kg (440 to 660 lbs). Immediately before entering the maternity den in the fall, the weight of a pregnant adult female can exceed 500 kg (1,100 lbs) because of the enormous amount of stored fat. At birth, cubs weigh only 600 to 700 grams (19 to 22 oz). The largest polar bear on record was a huge male, allegedly weighing 1,002 kg (2,200 lb); he was shot at Kotzebue Sound in northwestern Alaska in 1960.

did you know?

Why do some black bears have different colored markings on their chest? The markings on the chest, commonly called a chest blaze, can be a variety of shapes and sizes and are white or light brown in color. Not all bears have chest blazes. They can consist

of a small dash, a deep V, or a patch. While there is no way to be certain, the current theory is that these chest blazes are used for communication and identification among the bears themselves. Eighty percent of all cubs are born with chest blazes, but many lose them as they age. If the mother has a blaze, cubs are more likely to retain theirs as they age.

PHOTO: IRENE SHEPPARD   *[www.americanbear.org]*

Why Do Bears Hibernate?

Hibernation is a method to conserve energy when weather conditions are unfavourable and food is scarce. Bears that live in warm climates, such as Florida, often don't hibernate at all. In some areas where bears have learned that they can access non-natural foods, like garbage during winter, they are staying up year-round.

Most black and brown bears den for four to six months every year, entering the den in November or December and emerging in March or April. Unlike their more southerly cousins, polar bears do not hibernate in winter, with the exception of expectant mothers, who prepare a den and hibernate when pregnant to ensure that cubs are born in safety. The giant panda plus the spectacled, sloth, Asiatic black, and sun bears also do not hibernate because their food is available year-round.

Do other animals hibernate? Yup. Other hibernating mammals

include chipmunks, ground squirrels, echidnas, possums, hedge-hogs, hamsters, skunks, bats, prairie dogs, marmots, badgers, and some lemurs. Even some species of lizards, frogs, toads, newts, snakes, turtles, and insects, like bees, hibernate.

One bird, the Common Poorwill, is considered a hibernating bird. Other birds, like hummingbirds, may go into a state called torpor on a daily basis—their metabolism slows at night so they can rest and not require a constant intake of food to stay alive.

There have even been some interesting cases of people surviving exceptionally cold temperatures by falling asleep when their metabolism slowed just like it would in a state of hibernation.

Do bears wake up in the den? A bear can be easily awakened during hibernation. Since their bodily functions have only been lowered somewhat, they can wake up, shift their position, redistribute their bedding materials and keep their cubs in line.

What Is Hyperphagia?

Throughout autumn, hibernating bears prepare for denning by working overtime to pack on the pounds. As the bears' biological clock shifts, their appetites increase and they eat three times as much as they do during the summer. This exaggerated eating mode is called hyperphagia. The amount of time spent feeding each day increases to about 20 hours and they consume as many as 15,000 to 20,000 calories per day. The objective is to gain enough weight to make it through a four- to six-month snooze.

trivial but true

Gett'n Fat Is Where It's At! Bears in northern climates have only a limited time in which to build up fat stores in time for winter. Since they eat about 20,000 calories in a single day, that's roughly equivalent to eating 95 Taco Bell soft tacos or 30 Burger King Whoppers or 55 McDonald's chocolate shakes or 40 Dairy Queen banana splits! That would surely give us brain freeze!

Surviving Without Food

In order to survive without eating, bears must slow down their physiological systems and live off their fat reserves. They actually enter a state of dormancy where their heart rate drops from 40–70 beats per minute to 8–12 beats per minute; their metabolism slows down by half; and their body temperature drops by 3° to 7°C (5° to 13°F). While bears do not eat or drink during this time, they don't urinate or defecate either. Such a build-up of urea would cause humans to die. Bears, however, have the unique ability to recycle the build-up of urea, using its constituents to manufacture new proteins. During hibernation, the bear's body essentially enters a mode of conservation, efficiency, and recycling.

trivial but true

A Bad Fur Day During spring, a bear's coat is very matty and almost unhealthy looking. That's because they shed both their underfur and outer guard hairs, leaving only a short, sleek summer undercoat. They get rid of this old hair by rubbing against trees and rocks.

How Big Are Newborn Cubs and How Many Are Born?

In North America, cubs are born in the den during the coldest months of the winter—January or February. They are barely as big as squirrels when they are born. Litter size is usually two, but ranges from one to four or more cubs. The largest recorded litter

An 18-week-old bear cub. *PHOTO: SYLVIA DOLSON*

size is six. Cubs only weigh one-tenth as much as human babies, even though their mothers are much bigger.

What Is Delayed Implantation?

North American bears typically mate between May and early July. Although these bears have a gestation period of only six to eight weeks, birth doesn't actually occur until six months later in the dead of winter. How is this possible? Delayed implantation keeps fertilized eggs from developing into embryos until around the start of denning season. If female bears do not attain sufficient body fat or weight, the fertilized eggs will not develop. After a good food year, bears may produce litters of two or more cubs; after bad food years, they may only have one cub or none at all.

Grizzly Bear Cubs Nurse for up to Three Years

Grizzly bear cubs begin nursing when they are born in their

mother's den during hibernation. Newborn cubs will usually nurse for less than ten minutes every two to three hours. Grizzly cubs will continue to nurse for the next two to three years, depending on when their mother decides to wean them. Grizzly bear milk is roughly 30-percent fat. From an

Female grizzly bears have six nipples. This photo of a standing female grizzly bear clearly shows the four nipples on her upper chest. The two groin nipples (not visible) facilitate nursing when a mother grizzly bear is curled up in her den. If she had nipples in the center of her chest they would get lost in the folds of her curled up body while in the winter den. *[TEXT/PHOTO: JESSICA TEEL, WWW.GRIZZLYBAY.ORG]* early age, grizzly cubs also eat solid food; alternating between nursing, grazing on grasses and other vegetation, and eating insects (caterpillars or ants) and fish where available.

It is impossible not to notice when grizzly cubs are hungry. Wishing to nurse, grizzly cubs will begin to whine, which is a surprisingly deep type of howl or growl. If the mother doesn't respond promptly, the cubs will pursue her, becoming louder and more forceful to demand milk.

When grizzly cubs are actually nursing they make a voluble purring noise, sometimes called a "nursing chuckle." However, it sounds more like a loud, rhythmic fluttering noise than the purring you might associate with a cat. Like the fluttering of a thousand tiny wings, the noise is thought to encourage the mother to release milk. Cubs switch nipples often during nursing, and young cubs will also kneed the nipples with their paws to stimulate the flow of milk. Usually after nursing both mother and cubs will settle in for a long nap.

Mother grizzly bears nurse in a variety of positions, but most often they are either sitting up, or reclined onto their backs. While lying on their backs, most mothers keep their heads raised to remain vigilant, scanning left and right every minute or so for potential danger. *[Jessica Teel, www.grizzlybay.org]*

Why Do Bears Play?

Few animals play more than bear cubs do, but why they play remains a mystery. Scientists have suggested that young animals might play to practice fighting, mating, or hunting skills they will need as adults. Perhaps it's to help strengthen social bonds, reduce aggression, enhance alliances, increase tolerance, or improve group cohesion.

While these all sound like good ideas, none have been proven. There is no consensus on why young animals risk injury and burn up energy in carefree activities simply to have fun.

Play is most elaborate and prolonged in young mammals

Black bear cubs at play. *PHOTO: SYLVIA DOLSON*

whose behavior as adults is based in large part on learning—animals like bears, dogs, cats, and primates.

Some bear cubs play long and hard. Others play much less. Each has its own personality. Well-fed cubs play more than malnourished ones.

Unlike children, bears play without vocalizing. Cub play often looks like fighting, but fighting is noisy. Play is quiet and play-bites are gentle. Play often begins when a family reaches a puddle, an open field, or a soft pile of wood chips.

Bears play much less after they reach 18 months of age and are forced to leave the security of their mothers. Some siblings who played a lot when they were together as a family sometimes never play with each other again.

There are also circumstances that lead to play in older bears: during courtship, having cubs to play with, and where food is so abundant they don't have to spend all their time looking and competing for it. Most often, these play partners are unrelated adolescent males. Females seldom play with each other. Instead, they tend to be "territorial" competitors, even where food is abundant.

A springy tamarack sapling is also an invitation to play. Bears recognize these supple trees from a distance and run and jump on them. They climb up, ride the tops down, get off, and climb them again. They walk the bent-over trees like tightropes, and play "king of the mountain" with their mother and siblings. Bears eat nothing from these trees; they just seem to enjoy them. *[www.bear.org]*

How Can You Tell a Grizzly from a Black Bear?

Although the two species are similar in appearance, there are a number of physical traits that can be used to reliably distinguish black and grizzly bears in the field.

Many people rely on color and size, neither of which is a dependable feature. Color is not a decisive characteristic in distinguishing black and grizzly bears due to the great range of colors present in both species. Size is also not a dependable feature: while, on average, the grizzly is the larger of the two species, individual bears vary greatly in size. For example, a young grizzly will be smaller than an adult black bear. Other factors affecting size include age, sex, food availability, time of year and the location of populations. The following are reliable features to identify the species of bear:

Shoulder Hump/Highest Point While the grizzly's highest point when standing on all fours on flat ground is its shoulder hump, the black bear's highest point is its rear. The black bear does not have a pronounced shoulder hump. It should be noted, however, that the black bear may appear to have a shoulder hump in certain situations, such as when it is standing on a slope facing downhill or when its front legs are on a rock or log.

Facial Profile and Ears The grizzly has a concave or dished facial profile that extends from between its eyes to the tip of its nose. This dished-face profile of the grizzly makes its face appear broader and rounder when seen from the front. In comparison, black bears have a flatter, fairly straight, 'Roman-nosed' profile from their forehead to their noses.

Grizzlies' ears are much smaller than black bears' ears, and they are spaced farther apart. Keep in mind that young bears of both species have large ears in proportion to their head/body size.

Front Claws Grizzlies' front claws can be up to 10 cm (4 inches) in length and are usually light in color. Black bears have dark, curved claws about 3 to 4 cm (1 to 1½ inches) in length.

Distinguishing Features of a Black Bear

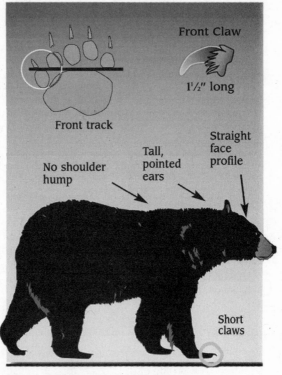

COURTESY OF CENTER FOR WILDLIFE INFORMATION
www.centerforwildlifeinformation.org

trivial but true

Why do grizzlies have a hump on their shoulders? Their hump is a large muscle mass used to power the forelimbs in digging. Grizzlies seem to dig more than any of the other species of bears and this powerful digging ability allows them to feed on roots, bulbs, and rodents; tear rotting logs apart for the protein rich bugs and grubs; and dig dens on steep mountain slopes. The grizzly's pronounced hump is an excellent distinguishing characteristic to tell black bears apart from grizzlies.

Distinguishing Features of a Grizzly Bear

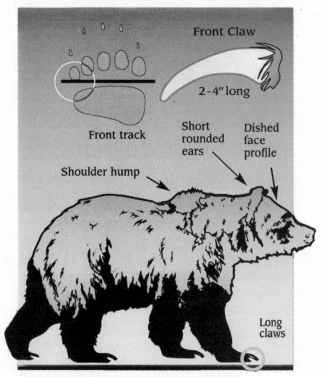

COURTESY OF CENTER FOR WILDLIFE INFORMATION
www.centerforwildlifeinformation.org

Why Are Grizzly Bears More Aggressive than Black Bears?

The two bear species have evolved different strategies for survival. Black bears have evolved to live in forests and thus are more likely to retreat to safe cover by climbing trees when threatened. On the other hand, grizzlies have adapted to life in treeless, open environments—with no place for retreat, they are more likely to defend themselves when threatened. Unlike the smaller, more agile black bear, adult grizzlies are also too large to escape danger quickly by climbing trees, so they respond to danger by standing their ground and warding off their rivals. But don't assume you can climb a tree to escape from a grizzly—if highly motivated, a grizzly will climb a tree too.

The Truth: How Dangerous Are Bears?

Most interactions between bears involve considerable tolerance and restraint. They usually display the same tolerance towards people. Bears prefer to avoid people whenever they can. In fact, most people never even know they are close to a bear before it vanishes into the forest. Each year countless interactions occur between people and bears without harm. A meeting...a mutual departure...no attacks, no injury, no news. But on rare occasions a meeting between a bear and a person results in human injury or death. Each year, on average, three people are killed in bear attacks in North America. Each year there are millions of interactions between bears and people in North America. The number of serious and fatal injuries is a very small fraction of these interactions. *[Staying Safe in Bear Country video]*

Bear attacks are rare and need to be put into perspective. The odds of being struck by lightning or killed by a bee sting are many times greater than being attacked and killed by a bear. In the United States, you are 67 times more likely to be killed by a domestic dog. For every person killed by a black bear, there are approximately 17 deaths from spiders, 150 deaths from tornadoes, 180 deaths from bees and wasps, 374 deaths from lightning, and tens of thousands of homicides. It is far more likely you would be killed in a vehicle accident on the way to the wilderness than by a bear. *[Dr. Lynn Rogers]*

Each year in the USA and Canada, 1 in 19,000 people commit murder; 1 in 35,000 grizzly bears kill a human; 1 in 700,000 black bears kill a human. *[U.S. DEPT. OF JUSTICE, STATISTICS CANADA, AND DR. STEPHEN HERRERO]*

Black and Grizzly Bears: Not Good Hunters

Black and grizzly bears are not efficient predators, primarily because their skeletons are designed for strength and power rather than speed, as is evidenced by their thick limbs, massive shoulders, and short backs. In addition, a bear's muscles are thick the entire length of the leg, rather than tapered towards the foot like a cat's. A thicker muscle close to the hip and shoulder improves speed, while a thick muscle mass stretching the entire length of the leg is equivalent to trying to run with weights on your feet! Longer metapodials, or foot bones, also increase stride length and improve speed, but bears have relatively short metapodials. *[www.americanbear.org]*

Any sizable prey is usually obtained in the form of the very young or very old, the sick or already deceased. Bears commonly overpower better hunters such as wolves and mountain lions and steal their food.

Yet, they're not designed to be vegetarians either. Although bears eat mostly vegetation, they don't digest it very well. The cells of many plants that bears eat are surrounded by a tough cell wall containing cellulose. Because of the chemical bonds that bind cellulose molecules together, cellulose is very difficult to digest, at least for most vertebrates including bears. Deer and cattle have solved the problem of cellulose digestion; they have multi-chambered stomachs that contain a soup of microorganisms that produce enzymes that can break the chemical bonds in cellulose.

Bears, however, have simple, one-chambered stomachs that do not contain cellulose-digesting microorganisms. Then how can bears make a living eating mostly vegetation? They rely on new, actively growing plants in spring and early summer. Young, fast-growing, succulent grasses and forbs do not contain a lot of cellulose, and therefore, they are much more digestible to a bear than are the same plants when mature.

Early growth plants are also nutritious. They can be as high as 20- to 30-percent protein on a dry-weight basis. As these plants mature, however, their protein content falls to as little as 3 or 4 percent. Young plants are adequate for maintenance of weight, but their high water content and limited

caloric content are not very good at building fat reserves needed by bears to survive the winter.

Gorge and store in the summer, and sleep and conserve in the winter. While bears can easily survive cold harsh weather, remember: they're not the best of hunters and prey is sparser and even more difficult to catch in winter. And we know that they also don't have the digestive efficiency to survive on low-nutritional plants. In winter, then, bears would expend more energy trying to catch the occasional prey and digesting nutritionally void plant matter than they would gain from these food sources. Nature and time have instead decided that it's best to gorge and store in the summer, and sleep and conserve in the winter. *[Jessica and John Teel, www.grizzlybay.org]*

Male grizzly scores a salmon at Glendale spawning channels (Knight Inlet, BC, Canada). *PHOTO: SYLVIA DOLSON*

trivial but true

Which bear has a thumb? The giant panda has a paw, with a "thumb" and five fingers; the "thumb" is actually a modified sesamoid bone which helps the panda hold bamboo while eating.

Are Bears Territorial?

In certain instances researchers have found some bears, usually females, to be highly territorial. An intruder would be chased away or even seriously injured by the female in residence. It would be nearly impossible for a male bear to defend a home range that could measure as much as 100 square miles. Males generally forgo territoriality and instead rely on a dominance hierarchy to keep social order. Bears announce their presence by scent marking—urinating, defecating, and rubbing, scratching and biting trees. More submissive bears will avoid areas where a dominant male is found. Occasionally, bears will even congregate at an abundant food source—examples are the salmon runs in the Pacific Northwest or open garbage pits. While squabbles may erupt periodically, their need for food overrides their natural fear of one another. [*www.bear.org*]

What Threatens Bear Populations?

Human activities pose many threats to bears and their environment: namely habitat loss, fragmentation and degradation; poaching and hunting; pollution; and human-induced climate change.

Bears are also killed by wildlife officials, ranchers, and farmers as a result of conflict with people, their property, pets and

Bears are sometimes trapped and relocated to areas away from human development. This rarely successful strategy is often used to appease the public. *PHOTO: SYLVIA DOLSON*

livestock. Roads and railways are another source of direct and indirect mortality for bears. Many are struck and killed by trains or vehicles, while other bears die because of the adverse effects roads and railways can have, especially when providing increased access for people to the backcountry.

Bears' low reproductive rates, and among some species, the long period of parental dependency, further contribute to their vulnerability. The elimination of just one spectacled bear, for example, may have a significant impact on populations made up of only a small number of individuals. In Peru, there are reports of inbreeding, resulting in decreased adult size and reduced number of offspring.

Global warming is considered to be the greatest threat to polar bears. Recent declines in polar bear numbers can be linked to the retreat of sea ice and also to the later formation of sea ice each year. With ice breaking up earlier in some areas, bears are being forced ashore before they build up sufficient fat stores, or forced to swim longer distances, which may lead to exhaustion and drowning. The consequences: thinner, stressed bears; decreased female reproductive rates; and lower juvenile survival rates. Polar bears are also hunted throughout most of their range. Although regulated in Canada and banned in Russia, illegal hunting is difficult to control and traditional subsistence hunting is unregulated. *[www.hsus.org]*

The poaching and illegal trade of bears and bear parts, including the Asian bear bile market, also contribute to shrinking bear populations. The illegal trade of wildlife in Thailand, for example, impacts both the sun bear and Asiatic black bear. Bear parts are openly sold in Chinese medicine shops throughout Asia, especially the gall bladders. Skulls and hides are also available. Bears are preferred as a special meal to enhance health and vigor by Korean tourists who visit Bangkok to eat in special restaurants. These restaurants procure bears for such meals and sometimes reportedly kill the bear in front of the guests to assure them of the authenticity and freshness of the meal.

Pet keeping also affects bears by creating a market for live bears, especially cubs which are sold in local markets, not just overseas, but in the United States as well. In Thailand, pets are usually given away or sold to restaurants when they get older and less manageable. Although the sale of bears and bear parts is illegal, the legality of pet bears, along with limited support of law enforcement preventing sale of wildlife, results in a continuing market for bears throughout the world. *[www.bearbiology.org]* ⌁

Why Are Bears Being Poached for Their Gall Bladders?

Unfortunately for bears, they are the only species with a gall bladder that produces fairly large quantities of bile, or bile salts, an ingredient that has been used in traditional Asian medicines for as long as 3,000 years. It is believed to cure a number of ailments, including cirrhosis of the liver, high blood pressure, jaundice, diabetes, heart disease, fever, headache, hemorrhoids, severe burns, and tooth decay. It also is used in health care products such as shampoo, and as a food delicacy. While synthetic forms of UDCA (the active ingredient in bile that has been proven to have some medicinal qualities) are available, there is a tradition that indicates the cure must come from nature to be effective.

Prices for bear gall bladders are astronomically high in some countries—in Japan, gall bladders can sell for $1,500 to $4,000 each. A bear gall bladder is approximately the size of a human thumb, and is virtually indistinguishable from the gall bladder of a cow or a pig in its dried, fig-like state. Fakes have flooded the market, leading some people to go to extraordinary lengths to obtain authentic gall bladders. This has led to an increase in poaching across North America and Russia. *[www.americanbear.org]*

What To Do If You See A Bear

Encounters with bears rarely lead to aggressive behavior and bear attacks are even rarer. There are no hard and fast rules when it comes to bears, but the following tips may help:

◆ Remain calm and assess the situation. Keep your wits intact and trust them.

◆ Stand still. Identify yourself as non-threatening by speaking in a calm, appeasing tone.

◆ You may move away slowly, preferably moving in the direction you came from. Do not run. In most cases, the bear will flee or even ignore you.

◆ If the bear is still off in the distance, try to make a wide detour or leave the area. Respect the bear's need for space. Never approach a bear, not even for a photo.

◆ Ready your deterrent (for example, bear pepper spray) and keep your group together.

◆ A bear may "pop" its jaws or swat the ground while blowing or snorting. It may lunge toward you or "bluff" charge in an attempt to motivate you to leave—usually stopping short of contact. These are defensive behaviors *(see pages 78 – 83 for more details)*, signaling you are too close. Remain calm and continue to increase your distance from the bear.

For more information, visit
www.bearsmart.com

Check the Recreating in Bear Country section.

PHOTO: SYLVIA DOLSON

FAMOUS BEARS

PHOTO: JON FREEMAN; COURTESY OF VITAL GROUND

The Legacy of Bart the Bear

Bart the Bear was no ordinary ursid. Born behind bars in a Baltimore zoo in 1977, Bart became one of the world's most famous bears, rivaling in his own way the likes of Yogi Bear and Winnie the Pooh.

When Bart arrived at the home of Doug and Lynne Seus, animal trainers from Park City, Utah, he was no bigger than a newborn baby, with feet smaller than the palms of Doug's hands. Bart was a Kodiak bear, and like his Kodiak brothers in the wild, he grew to be 9½ feet tall and weigh 1,500 pounds (which is about average for Alaska's coastal brown bears).

Over the years, Doug and Lynne trained Bart to appear in Hollywood movies. He was a smash hit. By the time he retired, he had appeared in fifteen feature films, seven television movies or episodes, fifteen documentaries, and had shared the stage with many great actors, including Dan Aykroyd, Alec Baldwin, John Candy, Anthony Hopkins, Brad Pitt, and Steven Seagal. In 1998, he even appeared on stage at the Academy Awards.

Although Bart was often called upon to play the role of the stereotypical monster—in *The Edge*, for instance, he tracks down and attacks Anthony Hopkins' character, and in *Legends of the Fall*, Bart actually "kills" Brad Pitt's character—Bart embodied those aspects of bears we don't see very often in the media. He was gentle, affectionate and loyal, and playful as a giant puppy. People who worked with Bart were constantly amazed that such a big, strong, ostensibly wild animal could be so attuned to the human beings around him.

Bart and Doug developed a strong bond during their 23-year relationship, not unlike the connection many of us share with our canine and feline companions. Doug had a unique ability to intuitively understand and communicate with Bart and the other animals he trained; an understanding that was reciprocated in turn by Bart. In "The Legacy of Bart the Bear," a short video available on YouTube, Doug and Bart can be seen wrestling as if they were brothers; the 1,500-pound bear being very careful not to crush his much smaller companion.

"To me he was a person," said Doug after Bart's death from cancer on May 10, 2000. "He was my soul mate...my comrade."

While many think Bart would have been better off in the wild, he seemed to have loved his job and adored the spotlight. He reveled in the praise of his trainer and the cheers and adulation of the film crew. "Bart knew when he was on camera," says Lynne. "It was like, 'Man, Bart, you're good.' And he was." Despite the fact he was thousands of miles from his ancestral Alaskan home, it seemed pretty clear that Bart the Bear had found his calling in life.

Bart died peacefully at his home in Utah at the ripe old age (for a bear) of 23. Although cancer took his body, his spirit lives on. While he was alive, Bart was the "spokesbear" for the Animal Cancer Center at Colorado State University and an ambassador for the Vital Ground Foundation, a Montana-based land trust that protects parcels of private land crucial to grizzly bear survival in Idaho, Montana, Alaska, and British Columbia.

Today, Bart's legacy lives on in a number of ways. Bart's successor, Bart 2, has taken over where Bart left off. A namesake Kodiak who was born in Alaska in 2000, Bart 2 has appeared in *Dr. Doolittle 2* and in TV episodes of *CSO* and *Scrubs*. He also played a prominent role in *Into the Wild*, a 2007 film about a young man's attempt to live a carefree life in the wilds of Alaska.

Bart's life in captivity allowed him to bring attention to important issues that affect animals—and bears in particular—everywhere. Thanks to the work of Vital Ground, many of Bart's wild brothers and sisters are able to roam free in habitat forever protected from development. To help remember Bart and protect habitat for all bears, consider making a donation to this important initiative at *www.vitalground.org.* ～

Feature Films
Windwalker, Pacific International Enterprises, 1980
Clan of the Cave Bear, Warner Brothers, 1984
The Bear, Tri Star Renn Productions, 1987
The Great Outdoors, Universal, 1988
Lost in the Barrens, 1989
Giant of Thunder Mountain, 1990
The Great American West, IMAX, 1991
White Fang, Disney, 1992
On Deadly Ground, Warner Brothers, 1993

Walking Thunder, 1993
Yellowstone, IMAX, 1994
Red River, Karvkeva Productions (French), 1994
Legends of the Fall, Tri Star, 1995
The Edge, 20th Century Fox, 1996
Meet the Deedles, Disney, 1997

Television Movies, Mini-Series and Episodes
The Gambler, CBS TV, 1983
Down the Long Hills, Disney, 1986
Lost in the Barrens, CBS, 1994
Lifestyles of the Rich and Famous, 1994
Young Riders, "The Decoy," MGM TV, 1995
Lonesome Dove/Deadman's Walk, ABC TV, 1996
McKenna, CBS, 1996
Academy Awards, 1998
SOURCE: www.vitalground.org

Bart 2. *PHOTO: KIFFIN HOPE*

Ancestral Bears

Modern day bears evolved from a smaller, dog-like creature (*Ursavus elemensis*) over 20 million years ago, when its home, in what we now call Europe, was a subtropical landscape and man had not yet arrived. Our ancestors, being small ape-like creatures, were still confined to the African continent.

It wasn't until about five million years ago that a creature readily recognizable as the ancestor of today's bears began to appear. At the time of this Auvergne bear, *Ursus minimus*, the world was already on the threshold of the Ice Age. In this much colder land, palm trees were replaced with deciduous trees and conifers. And far to the south, in Africa, a new sort of biped was already moving about on the ground, using sticks and stones to hunt small game. But the first encounter between man and bears as we know them today was still in the distant future.

About 2.5 million years ago, the Auvergne bear evolved into the Etruscan bear, *Ursus etruscus*. Over time, this species changed dramatically in size and behavior to become almost indistinguishable from what we know today as the modern brown bear.

Initially the Etruscan bear was small, like its ancestor the Auvergne bear. Likely a shy and reclusive bear, it was well adapted to life in the forest, consuming a diet of nuts, berries, insects, and small mammals. But as the climate cooled, glaciers advanced, and the world became a very different place. The bear, too, had to adapt in order to survive the colder climate and vast tundra left behind by the melting ice. With fewer trees, and dire wolves and sabertooth cats wandering around, it was no longer an advantage to be timid and reclusive. It paid to evolve into a bigger, tougher, faster animal.

The Etruscan bear eventually split into three evolutionary lines. One of the lines led to the European cave bear (*Ursus spelaeus*), a huge, largely herbivorous creature that towered above even the largest coastal brown bear. This immense bear has often been described as "the most bearish of bears" and was hunted by humans for thousands of years. It became extinct about 10,000 years ago.

A second line evolved to take advantage of life in the forest and eventually led to the evolution of the Asiatic black bear, *Ursus thibetanus*. This bear, in turn, led to the American black bear (*Ursus*

did you know?

Sibling Cubs Can Have Different Fathers Quite often, bear cubs in the same litter are only half-siblings. Sows (female bears) frequently mate with several different boars and are thus likely to bear a single litter of cubs fathered by multiple males. This benefits genetic variation in the population. *PHOTO: SYLVIA DOLSON*

americanus), whose ancestors appear to have arrived on the North American continent about 500,000 years ago, probably by way of a land bridge that existed between Alaska and Siberia during an earlier glacial period.

The earliest known fossils of the third line of evolution come from China. It is from these fossils that we can trace the evolution of the modern brown (grizzly) bear, *Ursus arctos*.

Roughly 200,000 years ago a number of brown bears living in Kamchatka became isolated by glaciers. The survivors underwent a rapid series of evolutionary changes in order to adapt to their new environment. This new brown bear subspecies became the first "polar" bear, *Ursus maritimus tyrannus*, which eventually evolved into the polar bear (*Ursus maritimus*). Brown and polar bears are still closely related and can, in fact, breed and successfully produce offspring.

And today, with global warming melting the polar bears' usual habitat on the ice floes, polar bears will likely find their way back to the land where they can hunt and forage for food. Unless there is a dramatic climatic shift, we might just witness polar bears devolving back to the grizzly species.

trivial but true

Why don't bears have long tails? Bears did have large tails, several million years ago! Since that time, the tail has been reduced to a small, furry flap of skin measuring only about 12 cm (5 inches) in length on a black bear. There are many folktales, stories, and legends that attempt to explain why the bear lost its tail. The scientific theory is far less exciting. It is believed that the bear lost its tail through the process of evolution, because it really did not need it. While dogs and other animals use their tails as a means of communication, bears tend to "face things" head on. Their display behavior often involves facing forward, either on two feet or four, leaving the tail practically invisible, and thus useless. [www.americanbear.org]

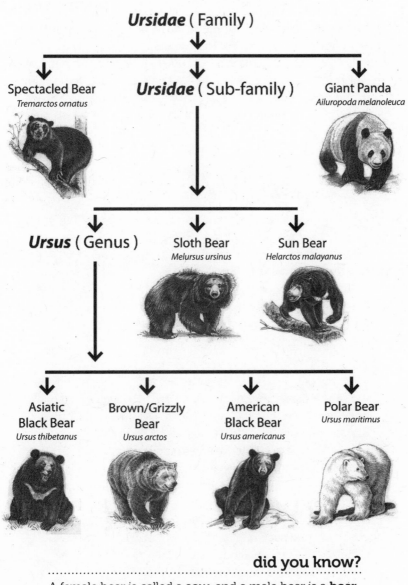

Ursidae (Family)

Spectacled Bear
Tremarctos ornatus

Ursidae (Sub-family)

Giant Panda
Ailuropoda melanoleuca

Ursus (Genus)

Sloth Bear
Melursus ursinus

Sun Bear
Helarctos malayanus

Asiatic Black Bear
Ursus thibetanus

Brown/Grizzly Bear
Ursus arctos

American Black Bear
Ursus americanus

Polar Bear
Ursus maritimus

did you know?

A female bear is called a **sow**, and a male bear is a **boar**.

trivial but true

Which of the following animals is not a bear: sun bear, koala, giant panda, red panda or sloth bear? Neither koalas nor red pandas are bears. A koala is a marsupial—just like a kangaroo or a wallaby. It has been nicknamed a koala bear due to its cute and cuddly appearance. The red panda, or lesser panda, is not a bear either—this small, red mammal is a member of the *Ailuridae* family.

Pizzly, Grolar Bear, or Nanulak?

A grizzly-polar bear hybrid is a rare ursid crossbreed that has occurred both in captivity and in the wild. In 2006, the occurrence of this hybrid in nature was confirmed by testing the DNA of a strange-looking bear that had been shot in the Canadian Arctic. Previously, the hybrid had been produced in zoos and was considered a cryptid (a hypothesized animal for which there is no scientific proof of existence in the wild).

While polar bear hybrids with Kodiak bears have been shot and reported in the past, DNA techniques were not yet available to verify the bears' genetic make-up. Jim Martell, a hunter from the United States, reportedly shot a grizzly-polar bear hybrid near Sachs Harbour on Banks Island, Northwest Territories, Canada on April 16, 2006. Martell had been hunting for polar bears with an official license and a guide, at a cost of $50,000, and killed the animal believing it to be a polar bear. Officials took interest in the animal after noticing its thick, creamy white fur, typical of polar bears, as well as long claws. Yet it had a humped back, a shallow face, and brown patches around its eyes, nose and back, and had patches on one foot—all traits of grizzly bears. If the bear had been adjudicated to be a grizzly, Martell would have faced a possible CAN$1,000 fine and up to a year in jail. A DNA test, later conducted by Wildlife Genetics International in British Columbia, confirmed that it was a hybrid with a polar bear mother and a grizzly bear father.

Canadian wildlife officials have suggested calling the hybrid "Nanulak," taken from the Inuit names for polar bear (Nanuk) and grizzly bear (Aklak). By another naming convention, the name of the "sire" would be ordered first, such that the offspring of a male polar bear and a female grizzly would be a "pizzly bear," while the offspring of a male grizzly and a female polar bear would be a "grolar bear."

did you know?

Genetically, is the polar bear most closely related to the sloth bear, brown bear (grizzly), or American black bear? Genetic research indicates that polar bears evolved from an isolated population of brown bears 250,000 years ago. Today, polar bears are considered marine mammals since they are highly adapted to life on sea ice. Their fur, short snout, and small ears are adaptations to the cold; their teeth are specialized for a completely carnivorous diet (primarily of Arctic seals); their feet have tiny papilae and "suction cups" for increased traction on ice; and their claws are shorter, sharper, and more curved than grizzly bears. Their body structure and locomotion is adapted to walking on ice and swimming between ice floes. If polar bears had to spend more of their lives on land, they would have to compete with grizzlies and other predators for prey for which they are not as well adapted.

did you know?

Bears are native to the continents of North America, Asia, Europe, and A) Africa; B) South America; or C) Antarctica?

Answer: B. Andean or spectacled bears are native to South America. There are no bears in Africa or Antarctica.

Bears and Humans 'Bear' Some Similarities

The body of the bear is disturbingly similar to the body of a human. When skinned, bears look rather like stocky, powerful, short-legged men. The bones of the front paws and feet of bears and people are so similar they have been confused in forensic circumstances. Bears can walk upright and, just like humans, have frontal binocular vision. Their hind feet are very human-like and the prints they leave in soft mud or melting snow can appear surprisingly like ones that might be left by a person. Bears are dexterous and can rotate their forepaws. There is even evidence that they may use tools. Aboriginal people also observed that bears snored when they slept, just like people. Like human mothers, bears have a strong maternal instinct. Bear cubs, especially grizzlies, stay with their mothers twice as long as other large mammals. *["Year of the Great Bear" by R.W. Sandford]*

Look at the lines that criss-cross your own human palm, or the soles of your feet, and see the similarities to the creases found on this back paw of a first-year cub.
[TEXT/PHOTO: JESSICA TEEL, WWW.GRIZZLYBAY.ORG]

PHOTO: SYLVIA DOLSON

Relationships with Humans

The relationship between bears and humans is a complex one. We have been sharing the landscape since modern humans wandered out of Africa some 60,000 years ago. Although there were no doubt conflicts between bears and aboriginal peoples in Eurasia and North America, bears, especially brown or grizzly bears, were treated with a great deal of respect.

In the northern forests, black bears were hunted for food, but grizzly bears were seldom targeted except for ritualistic purposes. In both cases, however, the killing of a bear was usually surrounded by elaborate myths and rituals. Hunters would fast for days before they went out, as a group, to bring their prey home. When they returned, the ceremonies often carried on for days afterwards as they celebrated the bear and the natural world of which they were all a part.

This relationship changed when European traders arrived. The coming of new technologies (such as the Sharps Carbine rifle) as well as new ideas spelled the end of the grizzly bear in much of North America. By the nineteenth century, trappers and hide hunters had extirpated the grizzly bear from much of its range. The arrival of more and more settlers "necessitated" the clearing of vast areas of prairie and forest, and wildlife of all sorts, including wolves and bears, were hunted mercilessly. Sustainability was never an issue because the goal was extermination. The survival strategies that bears had developed over millennia could not defeat the guns and sheer determination of an industrial culture.

The last known Great Plains grizzly in Canada was shot and killed near the Cypress Hills in 1883, though small populations of grizzlies would hang on in the hills and mountains of the central United States until the 1930s. By the time World War II ended, grizzly bears had been relegated to the northwest United States and western Canada.

Surprisingly, those who hunted bears for sport were also responsible for transcending the popular blood-thirsty image of the grizzly and dispelling many long-standing myths about aggression in bears. The first person to challenge the view of a grizzly bear as a ferocious man-eater, perpetuated by the famous American explorers Lewis and Clark, was Lieutenant Zebulon Pike. He wrote a letter to U.S. President Jefferson stating that the bears he encountered in the Rocky Mountain West did not attack unprovoked, but defended themselves vigorously.

At the beginning of the twentieth century, attitudes began to shift. National parks were formed to preserve some of the bear's remaining habitat, and laws were enacted and enforced to protect bears and other animals from exploitation. By the mid-1950s, many

trivial but true

Fast Food for Bears In the early 1940s, the Yellowstone Park dump was a bear-viewing hotspot. Staff would put garbage out for bears and the public would gather on bleachers to watch the spectacle.

An old Yellowstone National Park photo shows a bear begging for food.
PHOTO: R. ROBINSON

bears had become roadside attractions in parks and at garbage dumps. Rather than fearsome predators to be avoided or killed at all costs, bears had become a form of entertainment.

This created as many problems as it solved for bears. People in national parks were hand-feeding bears for photo opportunities. Easy access to high-calorie garbage and treats encouraged bears to seek out human food in campgrounds and residential neighborhoods instead of foraging for natural foods. As the boldness of hand-fed and food-conditioned bears increased, officials began killing animals that made a nuisance of themselves in order to protect the very people who had created the problem in the first place.

Toward the end of the last century, the public began to place a higher intrinsic value on protecting wildlife, and management policies started to reflect the shift in attitude. By the 1980s, feeding bears by hand or allowing them access to human food in garbage dumps was made illegal in national parks. Nonetheless, irresponsible waste management and selfish human actions persist to this day, resulting in thousands of dead bears every year.

Whether it's slaughtering bears to rid the land of inconvenient predators, hunting bears for sport, or removing bears involved in conflicts, the intentional killing of bears is abhorrent to many people. But arguably the biggest negative impact on bear populations in the last few decades has been the unrelenting destruction of bear habitat. Increasing human population and the increasing amount of urban, recreational, and industrial developments that accompany them continue to fragment bear habitat and stress bear populations. Putting humans and bears in close proximity results in more bear-vehicle collisions and more human-bear conflicts. Road access into wilderness areas results in increased hunting and poaching. Bears are simply running out of room.

Whether you regularly see bears near your home or on vacations, or if the only bear you ever see is the constellation Ursa Major, most of us still want bears to walk this Earth. We may disagree about how many bears are enough, or what they are really like, but we, and our world, would be poorer without them. ∽

Not far from the hustle and bustle of Whistler Village, a young black bear wanders alongside the ski runs of Whistler Mountain foraging on clover, grass and horsetail. Vegetated ski runs provide good spring forage and are often a great place to view black bears.
PHOTO: IRENE SHEPPARD

Legendary Bear Men

Grizzly Adams

James Capen Adams was a real-life legend of the American West who made his name in association with the grizzly. "Grizzly Adams," as he was known, arrived in California in the fall of the gold rush year of 1849 and began building a reputation as a collector and trainer of wild animals. By the mid-1850s, he lived with grizzly bears and other wild animals in his basement apartment on Clay Street in San Francisco. He became famous for having two bears, Lady Washington and Ben Franklin, with whom he used to walk in the streets of San Francisco. By the time Adams died in New York in 1860, he had established himself as a folk legend. *["Year of the Great Bear" by R.W. Sandford]*

William Wright

An American blacksmith, carpenter, sometimes-mailman, hunter and naturalist, William Wright spent a lot of time guiding hunting parties in Montana, Idaho, Washington, British Columbia and Alberta in the late 1800s and early 1900s. Over the course of his life, Wright admits to killing more than a hundred grizzlies. In one particularly ambitious day, Wright owned up to killing five grizzlies in five minutes with only five bullets. There is much about Wright's early attitudes toward hunting that would make him easy to dislike. What makes him different from many of the other renown bear hunters of his time is the evolution of his attitudes. Wright learned a great deal from his experiences, which transformed his opinion of bears. More importantly, in 1909 he wrote a book (*The Grizzly Bear: The Narrative of a Hunter-Naturalist*) about his observations that became the basis for a gradual but profound shift in the way the bear was viewed in North America. We owe a lot to William Wright. It was he who first suggested that photographing rather than hunting grizzlies was a superior way to learn about their behavior and appreciate their majesty. Wright also attempted to reshape the popular image of the great bear by explaining the context of its often "ferocious" behavior. *["Year of the Great Bear" by R.W. Sandford]*

Andy Russell

Andy Russell was something of a force of nature. Born in 1915, he was a hard-working rancher and guide-outfitter who became one of North America's most celebrated authors, wildlife photographers and filmmakers. Most of all he was a born raconteur and mountain man who loved all things wild—especially the grizzly bear, which he believed can "show us something of what it means to live in harmony with nature." He was the first to make a documentary film about grizzly bears in the wild *(Grizzly Country)*, which he made to dispel some of the myths about the grizzly bear. He followed that with a book of the same name and twelve others, and more than fifty articles and essays about his experiences in some of Canada's last remaining wilderness. His work garnered him numerous awards, including three honorary Doctorate of Law degrees from Alberta universities, the Golden Jubilee Medal, the Order of Canada, the J. B. Harkin Conservation Award, and, most recently, his induction into the Order of the Bighorn, Alberta's most prestigious conservation award.

trivial but true

Honey Bear Contrary to popular perception, bears are brood predators—which means they like to eat the bees, their pupae and larvae. The honey is only of secondary interest. That makes bears a serious threat to beekeeping operations, since they can do a great deal of damage to hives and equipment. It's best for beekeepers to erect an electric fence around the hives to keep bears out.

did you know?

Bears Have Highways Wherever you find bears, you will most likely find bear trails. It is common practice for bears to step in each other's footprints. Bear's paws have scent glands, and their footprints leave a scent trail. By stepping on top of a previous bear's tracks, a bear can place its scent on top of the previous bear's. Hundreds of years of footprints on top of footprints carve paths through the meadows and forests where bears live. *[TEXT/PHOTO: JESSICA TEEL, WWW.GRIZZLYBAY.ORG]*

trivial but true

Disorderly Conduct In August 2004, several news media outlets reported that a wild black bear was found passed out after drinking about thirty-six cans of beer in Baker Lake, Washington. The bear opened a camper's cooler and used its claws and teeth to puncture the cans. Apparently it selectively opened cans of Rainier Beer and left all but one Busch beer unconsumed.

Tips for Coexisting with Bears

◆ Keep your property free of bear attractants, which include bird feeders, fruit trees and berry bushes, dirty barbecue grills and drip pans, gardens, compost, and pet food.

◆ Store garbage and recycling securely indoors or in bear-resistant containers. Place curbside only on the morning of pick-up. Don't stockpile it.

◆ Keep accessible doors and windows in your home and vehicles closed and locked.

◆ Use deterrents to discourage bears from entering your property.

◆ If you encounter a bear in an urban area, make lots of noise to encourage it to leave.

◆ Help your neighbors to follow bear-smart practices.

Learn more at *www.bearsmart.com.* Another source for detailed information is Linda Masterson's book, *Living With Bears: A Practical Guide to Bear Country (www.PixyJackPress.com).*

PHOTO: SYLVIA DOLSON

PHOTO: JEAN CUMINGS

A bear was trapped inside the cab of this truck after breaking in for some empty food wrappers.

PHOTO: SNOWMASS VILLAGE ANIMAL SERVICES, COLORADO

Bears can enter homes through unlocked windows and doors looking for an easy food source. Once inside, they can cause a huge mess and significant damage. This is a great motivation for bear-proofing your home.

PHOTO: ANN BRYANT, LAKE TAHOE BEAR LEAGUE, WWW.SAVEBEARS.ORG

trivial but true

Staking Out His Territory The black bear is sometimes pursued by smaller animals. In newspapers on June 11, 2006, the Associated Press ran a photograph from West Milford, New Jersey, of a black bear treed by a woman's cat, a 15-pound tomcat named Jack. After she called the cat home, the bear descended from its perch, about 25 feet up in the tree, and ran off.

Bear Aware Groups Making a Difference

By the late 1990s, the needless slaughter of bears—whose only crime was seeking out an easy meal—motivated people all across North America to form "bear aware" and "bear smart" groups. Their mission: work with towns and their residents to keep food and other attractants away from bears, and work with wildlife agencies to mitigate conflicts in a non-lethal manner.

Their efforts are showing impressive results. For example, the Get Bear Smart program in Whistler, British Columbia, has reduced the number of conflict bears killed by over 50 percent despite a four-fold increase in the number of human-bear interactions. *[www.bearsmart.com]*

National and state parks are also doing their part. Bear incidents in Yosemite National Park are down 70 percent from 1998 to 2008, as a result of an extensive education, enforcement and a non-lethal bear management program. *["GreenPath" efforts, NPS Bear Patrol]*

Even some wildlife agencies are proactively confronting human-bear issues. The Colorado Division of Wildlfe formed Bear Aware in 1998 and has trained hundreds of volunteers to work one-on-one with homeowners, and businesses to prevent bear conflicts. *[www.wildlife.state. co.us/bears]*

It takes a community to live with bears, but "Nobody made a greater mistake than he who did nothing because he could only do a little." *- Edmond Burke*

PHOTO: CHRIS BENGE

To find programs in your area:
www.bearsmart.com/bearsBackyard/BearAwarePrograms.html

PHOTO: SYLVIA DOLSON

Primal Fear of Bears

Our image of bears is often shaped by common misconceptions that come from a lifetime of misinformation. One hurdle many people truly need to overcome is their innate fear of bears. The origins of this fear lie deep within the collective unconscious of our culture and have permeated our belief systems.

During the last century, civilized man developed an ambivalent love-hate relationship with bears. People are almost schizophrenic about bears. We love them and fear them; we are fascinated by them, yet wary at the same time.

Cute and cuddly teddy bears adorn children's beds, yet fierce and ferocious bears torment us in our nightmares. We love to see bears near us, but we prefer the safety of a secure, metal-enclosed vehicle between them and us, just in case.

In reality, bears pose only a very minor threat to human safety.

It is people who must overcome these fears before we can coexist together peacefully.

Bears have long suffered from an unearned bad reputation. According to bear biologist Dr. Lynn Rogers, wildlife danger is often highly exaggerated. Our views have been shaped by many things, including Hollywood movies, ferocious-looking bears on magazine covers, taxidermy mounts with unnatural snarls, and warnings written by government officials worried about liability problems. Legends, folklore, and even campfire stories are often embellished for entertainment value.

The media appeals to our primal fear with bold headlines about bear attacks, focusing our attention on a few rare attacks, rather than the thousands of incidents every year when bears avoided people. Sensational bear stories have always served to feed supposition at the expense of fact. According to a study done by Dr. Stephen Herrero and Andrew Higgins, the probability of a human suffering serious injury from a black bear or a grizzly in North America is greater than one in a million.

Misinterpretation of bear behavior, combined with a learned fear of these potentially powerful creatures, has unjustly put the bear on our most dreaded list. People often misread or misunderstand a bear's intentions. Bears

A black bear stands up to get a better sense of what caught his curiosity. *PHOTO: SYLVIA DOLSON*

cannot relate to humans by speaking English or French; instead they must use body postures, gestures and vocalizations to express themselves.

When black bears are hesitant or nervous near people, they may lunge and explosively expel air while slapping the ground or surrounding vegetation. Researcher Dr. Lynn Rogers and others have witnessed this startling and sometimes frightening display many times. Never, however, during years of study, has this display been followed by an attack. Rogers says it means the bear is uneasy and apprehensive.

Being face to face with a bear—despite a well-meaning attempt at rational thought—you may be overcome with fear. Unfortunately it is the bear that is most often the loser in these situations. Bears are usually killed, not for what they have done, but for what we are afraid they might do.

Black bears are actually very accepting of people and practice amazing restraint in their presence. They are extremely tolerant of humans and their actions, even when those humans misbehave or show poor judgment.

According to Rogers, "People often tell of close calls with dangerous wildlife. It's amazing, however, how many of those 'close calls' never ended in an attack. I prefer to characterize the black bear much more by restraint than by ferocity."

Enjoy the great outdoors and consider yourself fortunate to live on a planet where bears still inhabit the wilderness. ~

FAMOUS BEARS

Teddy's Bear

In 1902, American President Theodore "Teddy" Roosevelt went bear hunting in Mississippi. His hunting companions, concerned that the president hadn't had much luck, ran down a black bear with hounds. After one of the dogs was killed during the confrontation, the bear was cornered, clubbed and tied to a willow tree so that the President could shoot him. Roosevelt refused to kill the helpless animal himself, deeming it unsportsmanlike, but instructed that the bear be killed to put it out of its misery. *Washington Post* cartoonist, Clifford Berryman, immortalized Roosevelt's restraint in a political cartoon which caught the attention of a Brooklyn entrepreneur, Morris Michtom. Michtom's wife designed a toy bear and wrote to Roosevelt to ask if it might be named "Teddy's Bear," in the President's honor, to which he reluctantly agreed.

Even the politically astute Roosevelt could not have anticipated the success of the Teddy bear, but later decided to use one as a mascot in his bid for re-election. Since then, the Teddy bear has found its way into virtually every child's home. ～

A 1902 political cartoon by Clifford Berryman in *The Wahington Post* spawned the Teddy bear name.

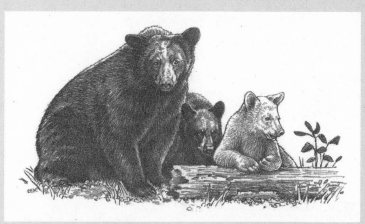

The Spirit Bear

The spirit bear, Kermode, is a unique subspecies of the North American black bear in which approximately one in every ten bears is white or cream colored. Some have orange or yellow coloration on their backs. Other Kermodes are all black.

The scientific name is *Ursus americanus kermodei*, named after naturalist and museum curator Frances Kermode of the British Columbia Provincial Museum. The term "Spirit Bear" is possibly attributed to a First Nations' tradition which credits these animals with supernatural powers and holds that the white bears were to be revered and protected. Today the Tsimshian people call it *moskgm'ol*, which simply means "white bear."

Kermode bears may have evolved on the northwest coast from a black bear population that became isolated from interior black bears more than 300,000 years ago. The white color may be due to inheritance of a single gene for hair color, but other more complex mechanisms may be involved. Further genetic research is needed.

Where Spirit Bears Live

The spirit bear is a unique creature. It lives only on the Pacific coast of British Columbia in Canada. Rarely a white bear is reported from other black bear populations elsewhere in North America, but these are from different subspecies.

The spirit bear is what scientists call an "umbrella species," that is, if a large enough suitable habitat can be protected for the spirit bear, many other species sharing the same ecosystem will also be protected under this umbrella, such as salmon, birds, wolves, deer, grizzly bears, insects, and many others.

Kermode family along a salmon stream in the new Spirit Bear protected area on the British Columbia coast. *PHOTO: W. MCCRORY*

trivial but true

Bearoscope Most North American bears are Capricorns or Aquarians since they are born from mid-January through early February.

New Spirit Bear Conservancies Still Need More Protection

In 2006, after an 18-year campaign spearheaded by the Valhalla Wilderness Society (VWS), the British Columbia government agreed to set aside nearly a half million acres of intact rainforest habitat to protect the spirit bear. A total of eleven conservancies have been legislated to achieve this, including a large area on Princess Royal Island, as well as other islands and large valleys on the mainland. Areas including Gribbell Island, and Green Inlet and Valley, where up to one third of the bear population is white-phased, still need protection.

Many other areas of the spirit bear's range—covering about one half of the British Columbia central and north coast—have, unfortunately, already been heavily logged. A promised new form of logging, called Ecosystem-Based, is supposed to protect bio-diversity. However, a review by VWS scientists shows that the new logging guidelines have been so watered down, as a result of lobbying from the timber industry, that they will not be enough. For example, this new type of logging will not adequately protect salmon-bearing streams nor the ancient trees that spirit bears (and grizzlies) rely on for their six-month period of winter hibernation, including "nursery" trees where young bears are born. VWS and others continue to engage in programs that will ultimately protect additional habitat critical to the spirit bear.

Take Action Now!

The Valhalla Wilderness Society needs your help—not just to save the spirit bear, but many other species, such as the mountain caribou in the British Columbia interior. See *www.vws.org*. ∿

THE VALHALLA

WILDERNESS SOCIETY

Do You Speak Ursine?

You may be more fluent in bruin vocabulary than you think. Communicating with bears is not unlike communicating with your pet dog or any other mammal. Bears convey their intentions through a diverse range of body language, vocalizations, and smells. You can read a bear's intentions by observing its body posture and listening to the tone of the sounds it makes.

When enraged, all animals make harsh sounds (loud guttural vocalizations); in contrast, they use soft-toned noises to make appeasement sounds.

We can all recognize that an animal that turns its back on us and ignores us likely means no harm. Whereas, if the animal is approaching us, we have to decide whether it's just plain curious or taking an assertive action to move us off. Usually, there are other telltale signs that help determine the animal's mood.

trivial but true

What do black bears and birds have in common? They are pigeon-toed. That means their toes point inward instead of straight ahead, making them excellent climbers.

A bear's ears are actually an effective way to recognize its emotions. Almost periscopic, a bear's ears are able to rotate and focus on different sounds. If the ears are pointing forward or upright (like Mickey Mouse's), the bear is usually at ease, and may feel curious or playful about something or someone. However, if a bear's ears are flattened against the head, this often means that the bear may feel threatened and may react aggressively. If the ears are simply twisted to the side or pointing backward, it's probably just listening to something beside or behind it.

A bear may stand up to get a better look and to sniff the wind—this is not a sign of aggression. But, they will let you know when you're making them feel uncomfortable. They may pause frequently to look up and see what you are doing—or they might make a huffing (expelling air loudly) or popping sound (clacking their teeth) or slap the ground signaling that you are too close for comfort. The "squared-off lip" is the switch (i.e. the lip is drawn forward and appears square; the face looks long) between a relaxed mood and these defensive postures.

Huffing, jaw popping, and slapping are all ritualized behaviors intended to intimidate an opponent—and, be assured, they work! Be respectful and heed the warning. Talk to the bear in a calm voice and make a wide detour around it.

You can also observe the position of the bear's head to judge his mood—if the head is purposefully held down low, it is often a sign of aggression. Sometimes, though, the bear may just be holding his head low in order to feed. Direct eye contact is another sign that a bear is exhibiting dominant behavior—if the eye contact is extended and almost piercing, the bear may be showing signs of aggression. If the bear is averting eye contact, or just glancing your way occasionally, then he is likely feeling nervous or apprehensive.

Be wary of a bear who walks toward you slowly, closing your comfort range, perhaps with his head held down lower than his shoulders. At this point, you know you have invaded that bear's personal space. To avoid an aggressive response, back away slowly without any eye contact and display as much disinterest as possible. Speak quietly and softly to indicate you are not threatening the bear.

The first line of defense for a bear is to bluff charge its rival—a full-tilt run, stopping short at the last minute. A bluff charge is almost always accompanied by previous ritualized behaviors, like huffing, teeth clacking or slapping the ground. Just before a more serious charge, a bear may lay its ears back and lower its body closer to the ground, fixing its eyes on the object of its aggression. Always remember, a bear normally prefers to bluff rather than risk injury to itself in a fight.

A startled grizzly may clack its teeth, turn sideways to show its body size, or make sudden short rushes at its contender.

More often than not, a bear just wants to go about the business of everyday life. A bear may sit down or move away to show

did you know?

Bear Claws Each bear paw has five long, strong claws used for tearing, digging, and climbing. Black bears have more tightly curved claws for climbing; grizzlies have longer, blunter claws for digging. A grizzly's claws can grow up to 13 cm (5 inches) in length on the fore paws. The hind-paw claws are always shorter than the forepaw claws. A polar bear has sharp, black claws that can grow up to 7 cm (2¾ inches). They are shorter than the grizzly's claws, but pointier. This extra sharpness provides traction on ice.

black bear claws   grizzly claws

respect. It may look away, yawning with feigned disinterest. It may exhibit "ignoring" behavior—standing motionless or perhaps grazing, indicating it has no intentions and just wants to be left alone. That doesn't necessarily mean the bear has lost its fear of humans, just that it's realized that these humans don't pose any immediate threat and it can relax. *[Ben Kilham, Dr. Stephen Stringham]*

NOTE: To better understand more offensive bear postures, please refer to Dr. Stephen Stringham's book, *Alaska Magnum Bear Safety Manual*. Chapter 10 provides detailed information on assessing bear moods and intentions as well as coping with aggression. ∼

Inhibiting Aggression

One reason that bears perform ritualistic or intentional displays is to inhibit aggression. Because bears occupy very extensive areas and meet face-to-face infrequently, the ritual use of chomps, huffs and false charges actually serves to deter attacks that might otherwise occur if these displays were lacking. Humans and other animals also have rituals to repress aggressiveness. For example, we may greet a strange dog with a slow approach and a kind word—while observing the response. If the response is friendly (such as a wagging tail), we may choose to pet the dog. If, on the other hand, the dog growls and bares its teeth, we would likely refrain from trying to pet the dog. Similarly, we might offer a smile or a handshake to strangers or people we haven't seen for a while. This gives us an opportunity to gauge the response of the individual we just met and react accordingly. Granted, the bear's rituals of snorting, chomping, huffing and false charging are not as cordial as ours, but both serve the same purpose—they inhibit potential aggressiveness and buy some time in order to gauge the situation. *[Ben Kilham]*

Can You Guess What These Bears Are Communicating?

Look closely at the eyes, ears and body. Match each picture to a message listed on the next page. *(Answers on page 84.)*

A.

B.

C.

D.

trivial but true

What animals have a black tongue? Polar bears. Even their skin is black. Chow dogs and giraffes have black tongues too, as well as some parrots, lizards and snakes.

E.

F.

1. Move away! ___
2. I smell something ___
3. I'm content ___
4. I hear something ___
5. I'm curious; I might smell or hear something ___
6. I feel defensive ___

trivial but true

How long can a polar bear stay underwater? The polar bear can stay underwater for about two minutes—with open eyes, closed nostrils, and ears flattened against its head. They are excellent swimmers, capable of paddling up to 10 kilometers per hour (6 mph), and have been seen on ice fields over 160 kilometers (100 miles) from the nearest land.

What do polar bears eat in the event of a seal shortage? They seek out rabbits or Arctic foxes, or go through landfills or garbage cans if they live nearby humans.

Ever Wonder How a Bear Picks Berries?

The secret is in a bear's lips. Unlike humans' lips, which are attached to our gums close to our teeth—bears' lips are large and extend greatly away from their teeth. Their lips are highly dexterous and can be used to grasp and manipulate objects—much like humans use their fingers and thumbs. We tend to define an "opposable thumb" as a physical feature which distinguishes "higher" animals from "lower" ones because a thumb can assist with the use of tools and manipulation of an animal's environment. However, bear anatomy shows that nature can come up with a completely different design for accomplishing a similar task—like grasping. Bears use the dexterity in their lips for all sorts of food-related tasks, such as efficiently and quickly gathering and eating berries, breaking apart pine cones to extract the fatty seeds inside, or scooping out the high-fat eggs from inside the ripped-open belly of a fish. Did you know that a bear's tongue can reach six inches out of the mouth as it picks ants or berries? [Jessica Teel, www.grizzlybay.org]

PHOTO: SYLVIA DOLSON

ANSWERS to Pages 82 – 83

1. Move away! **C.**
2. I smell something **A.**
3. I'm content **E.**
4. I hear something **B.**
5. I'm curious; I might smell or hear something **F.**
6. I feel defensive **D.**

did you know?

Do bears walk in a plantigrade (flat-footed, like people) or digitigrade (walking on their toes, like cats and dogs) manner? Bears walk with plantigrade locomotion, meaning they walk with the podials and metatarsals (the soles of the feet) flat on the ground. Like humans, bears first strike the ground with their heels, and then roll forward to the balls of the feet and then to the toes. That's different than most carnivores which tend to walk on their toes in a way that is well adapted for speed. A bear's characteristic shuffling gait results from this plantigrade, flat-footed walk, but also because the hind legs are slightly longer than the forelegs. Another reason for the apparent shuffle is that they commonly walk with a pacing gait. Unlike many quadrupeds, the legs on one side move together instead of alternating, much like a pacer horse. *[Jessica Teel, www.grizzlybay.org]*

PHOTO: SYLVIA DOLSON

Do Bears Roar?

Not really, although they do make loud gutteral sounds and huffing noises. Often the sounds that bears make in Hollywood movies are dubbed-over lion roars. Even in documentary films, fight scenes are usually silent play-fights over-dubbed with sensational roars. The public has been routinely misinformed. Bear safety is not show business, and knowing about bears, how they react and how they sound during an encounter can help you deal with the situation.

FAMOUS BEARS

Yogi Bear

Yogi Bear was the most popular television cartoon creation of TV's early years. Created by William Hanna and Joseph Barbera, the "Yogi Bear" cartoons first appeared as a component

PHOTO: W. KELLER, NATIONAL PARK SERVICE

segment of *The Huckleberry Hound Show* in 1958. An inhabitant of Jellystone National Park, with his little bear buddy, Boo Boo, Yogi was for the most part a sarcastic, rule-breaking bear with a great yearning for pic-a-nic baskets who credited himself as being "smarter than the average bear."

Besides speaking in rhyme, Yogi will long be remembered for his many catch phrases including "Hey, Boo Boo!" and "Hello, Mr. Ranger Sir."

Yogi's personality and mannerisms were based on Art Carney's Ed Norton character on *The Honeymooners*. ～

trivial but true

How did Yogi get his name? Yogi was named after legendary New York Yankees catcher, Yogi Berra.

A black bear wears a remote-download GPS radio collar. *PHOTO: SYLVIA DOLSON*

Bear Detectives

Like detectives in a crime lab, biologists gather clues and evidence in the field to learn more about bears.

Tracking Bears

When biologists want to know detailed information about where bears go and what they do, they catch a bear in a live trap or snare, tranquilize it, and put a radio-collar around its neck. While the bear is tranquilized, biologists will often weigh it, take body measurements, hair, tissue or blood samples, and ear-tag it for identification purposes. After the bear is released, the radio collar sends out a radio signal (called a VHF signal, which is a pulse of steady beeps). The signal is picked up by a receiver and biologists can track the movement of the bear. If a bear lives in a remote area, or if several bears in one area are collared, biologists may use a GPS collar. GPS collars also emit a VHF signal, but they can be programmed to locate themselves via satellite as often as the biologist chooses, usually hourly. The location data is then retrieved from the satellite and translated to points on a map. When a bear spends more time in one area (if it is feeding or sleeping), biologists can go out in the field and do a site investigation after the bear leaves to look for clues about the bear's behavior and what habitat types are important. A biologist might find an ant colony ripped open, plants dug up or grazed on, a day bed, some scat, or other bear signs, like a mark tree. All of these clues help biologists build a picture of what bears do and where they do it.

Hairy Clues

Biologists even use DNA evidence to estimate the size of bear populations and their genetic make-up. The scientists set up barbed wire in areas where bears travel frequently. When the bear rubs against the wire, it leaves behind a few strands of hair. The hair is carefully packaged and sent to the lab where scientists can determine the number of unique individuals as well as their relatedness to each other. Fascinating stuff! *["Discovering Black Bears," Dog-Eared Publications]*

Dropping Clues

By examining scat, biologists can tell how long ago the animal passed through the area, the approximate size of the animal, and clues as to what it has been eating. Sometimes hair is found—it may be the bear's own hair from grooming or it may be the fur of a small mammal the bear has eaten. Spring scats usually consist of grass and clover, as well as other plant material. During the summer, scats reveal the many different kinds of berries that bears love so much. Scats may also contain nuts, seeds, insects or remnants of fish.

Bear scat often contains human food waste and garbage, including plastics and Styrofoam. Consuming these items can cause tragic results for the bears. Of all inedible material, plastics are the most frequently ingested (when bears consume garbage) and can cause blockages along the intestine, often causing death. Styrofoam can absorb important bodily fluids and/or act as an abrasive against the intestinal wall. The consumption of abrasive foods or pointed items can perforate the intestine, which may lead to intestinal inflammation and infection causing septic shock and agonal death.

Mark Trees

The type and amount of "sign" that bears leave in forested or open habitats varies among species. Many forest-dwelling bears leave scratch marks on both conifer and deciduous tree

What did these bears eat?
Top: grass. Bottom: bird seed.
PHOTOS: SYLVIA DOLSON

trunks to advertise their presence. Tree marking behavior occurs frequently along bear trails, ridge tops, and abandoned roads. Although the function of these mark trees is not known, researchers have documented that the marking behavior is more prevalent during the breeding season, suggesting that it may play a part in the reproductive ecology of bears. However, marking behavior also occurs during the non-breeding season, so it is not completely associated with breeding activities. Bears often advertise their

trivial but true

1. Guess how many raspberry seeds one biologist found in a pile of bear scat? A) 100; B) 1,500; or C) 3,000

2. How many hazelnuts did a black bear eat in one day?
A) 56; B) 809; or C) 2,605

Answer #1: fifteen hundred; #2: twenty-six hundred and five

[*Discovering Black Bears*; Dog-Eared Publications]

marks by taking advantage of the aromatic qualities of trees—by biting into the bark and letting the sap emerge and blend with their own scent and hair. Biting off the tops of softwoods is common. *[Dr. John Beecham, Ben Kilham]* ～

A mark tree at the end of a stomp trail. Bears turn their back, rub the tree, and often bite the bark. *PHOTO: DAVID KRUGHOFF, WWW.PHOTO ARTCANADA.COM*

Bears often leave scratch marks on trees inadvertently while they are climbing. In time, the scratch marks become embedded in the bark and will grow deeper and wider. Fresh marks can be identified by loose bark fragments.

trivial but true

Green Bears? Is it true that polar bears at the San Diego Zoo turned green? Yes. After the coats of three adult polar bears turned markedly green in the summer of 1978, a study of their fur revealed that the unusual color was caused by algal cells living inside the wide, hollow guard hairs of the bears' outer coats. This phenomena is apparently unique to captive polar bears.

Bears' Teeth: Clues to Their Age and Diet

[Adapted from *Discovering Black Bears*; Dog-Eared Publications]

How is a bear's tooth like a tree stump? A bear's teeth grow continuously throughout its life. In fact, if scientists want to know how old a bear is, they extract a small tooth, cut it in half and count the rings. Well, they have to send it to the lab to look at the rings under a microscope, but it's that simple. Scientists can tell which years had plentiful or scarce forage just by the size of the ring. In good food years, the spaces between the rings are wider than in bad food years. The space is narrower in years when a mother has cubs as most of her energy is diverted into milk production. The dark lines are laid down in the winter while the bears are mostly inactive.

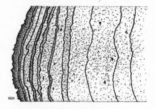

How old is this bear?
16 years of age.

Teeth Reflect Diet Grizzly and black bears are omnivores and their 42 teeth reflect a diet of both plant material and meat. Different teeth were designed for different jobs. Molars are for grinding and chewing plants. Canines are for stripping bark, leaving marks in trees, and tearing apart wood. Their teeth also fit together like scissors allowing the canines to tear apart flesh. The open area, or gap, where branches can be pulled through to strip leaves is the diastema. Incisors in the front of the mouth are used for grabbing, chomping, nibbling and tearing.

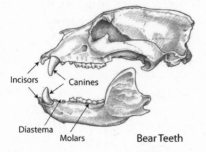

Incisors
Canines
Diastema
Molars
Bear Teeth

The Bear as a Healer

In many aboriginal cultures, the bear was revered as a great healer because the bear knew the secrets of the plants. Often portrayed as the plant gatherer in many Native myths, the bear is seen as a mysterious herbalist gathering medicines straight from nature's pharmacy. Even the names of many North American wild plants, such as bear's tongue, bear's wort, bear's tail, bear's paw, bear clover, bear's ear, bear's breech, bear moss, bear corn, bear bane, and bearberry reflect the bear's widespread association with medicine and healing.

North American black bears and grizzlies are known to dig up *Ligusticum porteri* (also known, not surprisingly, as bear root or osha), chew the root into a mash and rub the paste through their fur. As they do so, they go into a catnip-like frenzy, often growing calmer after a session with the root. Bear root is very effective as an antiviral and antipeptic (digestive aid), and is known to have antibiotic properties—making it an effective treatment for stomach aches and bacterial infections. It may also offer bears relief from fleas, ticks, and even fungus conditions. As an all-round painkiller, humans use this medicinal plant for rheumatism, arthritis, and sore muscles. It's also been discovered that there are steroids, cardiac glycocides, and coumarins within the bear root plant—a group of important natural compounds that have been found to have numerous healing properties.

Bears often rub on resinous trees such as pine. They seem to love utility poles freshly painted with creosote. Their preference for these smelly substances may be related to the immediate relief of itching from biting flies and ectoparasites (parasites that live outside the body). The resins impair the health of mites, lice and ticks; repel biting insects; and are anti-microbial, helping heal bacterial and fungal infections. Or, the bear may just be scratching an itch or leaving its mark.

Bears may even rid themselves of tapeworm and intestinal parasites by eating a rough fibrous sedge (*Carex spp*) before going into hibernation.

Like many other mammals and birds, bears consume clay—a practice known as geophagy. Clay-licking may help bears feel better when infested with intestinal worms or poisoned by natural dietary toxins.

Bears sometimes chew on ash, perhaps to settle their stomachs. The largest volcanic eruption in the twentieth century occurred in Katmai National Park in Alaska. Much of the park soil is volcanic ash and the bears eat this ash—it's a natural form of antacid. This makes a lot of sense, given that meat/fish and nuts

The Science of Zoopharmacognosy

According to researchers in the relatively new science of zoopharmacognosy (animal use of medicinal plants to treat illness), several species of animals are known to seek out plants that have known medicinal properties.

Many of us witness this with our own pets—dogs and cats eat grass to aid with digestion. Some monkeys in Brazil eat a fruit that may function as a fertility drug. Birds do "anting"—the rubbing of live ants on their feathers, presumably relying on the insects' defensive secretions as natural fungicides or insecticides. Rats that eat clay can survive an otherwise lethal dose of pesticides. And chimpanzees seek out plants that act as treatments for intestinal parasites.

(at times the bulk of a bear's diet) are highly acidic foods. The ash also helps to get rid of parasites in the digestive tract. *[Jessica Teel; www.grizzlybay.org]*

According to Benjamin Kilham, who raises orphan black bears in the wild, when one of his bears named Yoda suffered an infection as a result of a fighting wound, she dug a cool, wet den in a wooded swamp and crawled in it for five days, possibly to fight the corresponding fever. Squirty, another of Kilham's rehabbed orphans, seems to have figured out that citronella would keep the deer flies from her ears. She now uses her paws to rub her ears in the citronella that Kilham applies to trees in order to attract bears for research purposes.

Bear biologist Dr. Lynn Rogers puts out piles of cedar chips for bears in the spring. The strong smell of cedar is known to repel insects. According to Rogers, "We speculated that the chips might help bears get rid of mites or other pests, like cedar chests repel moths. We don't know for certain if that is the attraction, though, or if bears just like to play in cedar chips more than in other kinds of chips."

Certainly, more research is needed to prove scientifically whether bears or any animal uses various substances for medicinal purposes, but it's hard not to wonder.

Bears May Hold Secrets to Medical Mysteries

Can astronauts on long space voyages benefit from sleeping bears? To survive long winters, bears hibernate, or go into a deep sleep, usually for four or five months. If humans were to lie still for that long, their bones would weaken and their muscles would waste away. If scientists can figure out how hibernating bears stay strong, they could find a way to help astronauts who can't do weight-bearing exercise in the weightless environment of outer space. They could also help millions of people who are confined to beds or wheelchairs or suffering from diseases such as osteoporosis (the loss of bone density that comes with age). Even patients with kidney problems and heart disease could benefit from a better understanding of the bear's unique physiology.

During hibernation, bears do not defecate or urinate. Such a build-up of urea would cause humans to die, but bears have the unique ability to convert urea back into the building blocks of protein. Just how bears do this is a mystery that scientists think may be solved in the near future. The answers may help humans who need to use kidney dialysis machines.

Surprisingly, when bears hibernate, their heart muscles take on very similar characteristics to certain forms of human heart disease. Yet in the spring, bears' hearts quickly recover to normal activity. Through further study, scientists hope to learn more of how bears work their magic and what might help humans recover from heart disease.

Just as exciting is another recent discovery. During hibernation, a bear's metabolism slows down by half, its heart rate drops from fifty beats per minute to ten beats per minute, and its body temperature drops by 3° to 7°C (5° to 13°F). Scientists have learned that there is a substance responsible for these metabolic adjustments in bears as well as other deep hibernators. They think that the substance may have applications in human medicine—in particular, the survival of organs for transplantation surgery. At

did you know?

Liver Kills! If you eat a polar bear liver, you will suffer from vitamin A poisoning and might even die. The polar bear feeds largely upon fish-eating carnivores and thus ingests large amounts of vitamin A, which is stored in its liver.

present, 15 to 20 percent of all human donor organs have to be discarded as a result of deterioration. Any method that prolongs organ survival means that more transplants can occur and more lives can be saved.

Scientists are even researching the possibilities that the substance that makes animals hibernate (Hibernation Induction Trigger or HIT) may have applications in the treatment of insomnia, obesity and anorexia nervosa. Cancer and viral infections, like the common cold, have also responded well to HIT. *[Dr. Wayne Lynch]* ~

trivial but true

Killed for what? The sun bear is the least known of all the world's bears—and probably the most endangered. Habitat loss is a major threat, but so is man. Despite being on the endangered list, why are these creatures often deliberately shot?

A) They threaten valuable orchards.

B) Their teeth fetch a hefty price on the Asian black market when ground into a powder.

C) They are considered dangerous.

D) They live almost exclusively on flightless birds and will kill farmers' chickens.

Answer: A. The sun bear *(see page 24)* often eats the heart of coconut palm trees and that kills the tree. Orchard owners often kill the animals to protect their plantations.

Medicine Bear

It was out of the bear's remarkable capacity for self-healing that the legend of the Medicine Bear emerged. Medicine Bear is the spirit of bear or "healing presence." Healers from virtually all cultures within the bear's range work with spirit helpers, like the great bear, to uncover the wisdom to restore humans' physical and spiritual well-being.

A black bear cub of the year rests in the safety of a tree while mom forages below (Whistler Mountain, BC, Canada). *PHOTO: SYLVIA DOLSON*

Black bear young are left to fend for themselves at about 17 months of age. This brown-phased black bear has already been separated from his mother. (Whistler Mountain, BC, Canada). *PHOTO: SYLVIA DOLSON*

trivial but true

Worldly Bears There are eight species of bears in the world: American black bear, brown bear/grizzly, polar bear, Asiatic black bear, spectacled bear, sloth bear, sun bear, and giant panda.

A mother black bear tries to catch a few zzz's while her cub plans his next move (McCreery, Manitoba, Canada).

A 600-pound male black bear cools off in the summer heat (northern Minnesota).
PHOTOS: DAVID KRUGHOFF, WWW.PHOTOARTCANADA.COM

A young black bear cub stands up to get a better sense of whatever caught her attention (Whistler Mountain, BC, Canada). *PHOTO: IRENE SHEPPARD*

did you know?

Bears Are All Individuals Bears are highly intelligent and curious animals with complicated emotions that are in many ways different from human emotions, but nonetheless quite complex. Each and every bear has a very distinct personality, just as humans do, and no two bears are alike. That's why, in almost all cases, stereotypes and generalizations are inappropriate. Some bears are smarter, some are friendlier, some are more curious and some are more aggressive.

Jeanie, a beloved black bear of Whistler, trees with her cub, Jake, to avoid the activity below (Whistler Mountain, BC, Canada). *PHOTO: SYLVIA DOLSON*

did you know?

Not All Black Bears Are Black Black bears can be black, blue-black, dark brown, brown, cinnamon and even white. Grizzlies, likewise, may range in color, from black to blond, making it hard to distinguish the two species by color.

While these cubs are the same color as their mothers, that's not always the case—siblings can be different colors (black bears, Whistler Mountain, BC, Canada). *TOP PHOTO: JUSTA JESKOVA, WWW.COASTPHOTO.COM; BOTTOM: SYLVIA DOLSON*

A black bear comfortably perches on Western Hemlock boughs (Whistler Mountain, BC, Canada). *PHOTO: IRENE SHEPPARD*

This black bear almost looks like a grizzly with her shoulder fur puffed up by the wind (Blackcomb Mountain, BC, Canada). *PHOTO: SYLVIA DOLSON*

A black bear at Whistler Mountain, BC, Canada.
PHOTO: SYLVIA DOLSON

did you know?

Señor Bruin Bears can reach an age of 30 years or more, but only if they're really lucky. Most bears die much earlier than that at the hands of man, almost always needlessly.

Pushing 20 years of age, this Minnesota male black bear likely tips the scales at over 700 pounds. *PHOTO: DAVID KRUGHOFF, WWW.PHOTOARTCANADA.COM*

A large male grizzly intent on finding a mate (Hallo Bay, Alaska). *PHOTO: SYLVIA DOLSON*

Grizzly cubs stay with their mothers for two to three years. In some areas, mothers keep their young for four to five years (Hallo Bay, Alaska). *PHOTO: SYLVIA DOLSON*

trivial but true

'F' for Productivity! Bears are among the least productive mammals in Canada. In theory, if a male and female black bear born this year breed as soon as they reach sexual maturity and as often as possible, and if their offspring did the same, they could, in the space of ten years, grow to a population of just fifteen bears, assuming none died. Grizzly bears are even less productive: in 10 years, a male and a female born today could grow to a population of only eight. By comparison, a pair of white-tail deer could produce more than 1,400 descendants in 10 years. Oh deer!

Grizzlies of Hallo Bay, Alaska. *PHOTOS: SYLVIA DOLSON*

A good catch for this yearling grizzly (Glendale spawning channels, Knight Inlet, BC, Canada). *PHOTOS: SYLVIA DOLSON*

did you know?

What purpose does the fur serve? A bear's fur consists of two types of hair—the underfur and the outer guard hairs. The underfur is soft and dense and serves primarily as an insulator. The outer guard hairs are much thicker, longer and coarser. While they insulate, they also serve to protect the body from dirt, debris and insects. In addition, guard hairs repel water—when a bear emerges from a lake or creek, it will shake just like a dog shakes water from its coat, leaving it practically dry. *[www.americanbear.org]*

Giant panda in Wolong, China (*Ailuropoda melanoleuca*, literally "cat-foot black-and-white"). *PHOTO: DON REID, WILDLIFE CONSERVATION SOCIETY*

trivial but true

Bamboozled! Since a panda can't digest plant material as efficiently as a goat or a cow, it makes up for this inefficiency by eating very large amounts of bamboo. A panda can eat up to 39 kg (85 lbs) of bamboo each day. **Is the giant panda the only animal that depends on bamboo?** No, but only a handful of animals are predominantly dependent on bamboo, including the red panda, bamboo lemurs found in Madagascar, and bamboo rats in China and Southeast Asia.

Above: One-year-old panda cubs at Wolong Pandas Reserve in Wolong, Sichuan, China. *PHOTO: WWW.PANDASINTERNATIONAL.ORG* Below: A giant panda at the Beijing Zoo, China. *PHOTO: GREGORY MCNAMEE*

trivial but true

It's a girl...no, it's a boy? People can't tell if a baby panda is a girl or a boy for four years.

trivial but true

Retractable or Non-Retractable Claws? Unlike cats, bears' claws are non-retractile, so they can't hide them the way a cat does. As a result, a bear's claws are not as sharp as a cat's, whose claw retraction preserves their sharp points from wear.

Above: A young female grizzly squares off her lip in a defensive posture after she is disturbed by a cracking sound in the distance (Hallo Bay, Alaska). Below: A mother grizzly stands up to get a better look at an approaching male bear (Lake Clark National Park and Preserve, Alaska). *PHOTOS: SYLVIA DOLSON*

Above: Two male grizzlies spar over a female during mating season. Below: The winner makes tracks toward the female (Hallo Bay, Alaska). *PHOTOS: SYLVIA DOLSON*

A black bear cub climbs a tree above a ski run at Whistler Mountain, BC, Canada.
PHOTO: SYLVIA DOLSON

A dramatic rescue ensued after a hiker spotted a black bear hanging on for dear life from the Rainbow Bridge near Truckee, California.

The bear likely jumped over the side when she got spooked by traffic. Instead of free-falling 100 feet to a steep, rocky ravine below, she miraculously managed to hoist herself into a small crevice under the bridge.

With a tranquilizer gun and a huge net secured onto the bridge, a five-hour rescue mission was led by the BEAR League of Lake Tahoe with help from Truckee Animal Control. After the groggy bear was finally pushed into the net, she was lowered to safety and walked away unharmed.

PHOTOS: KELLIE BAKER, BEAR LEAGUE OF LAKE TAHOE, AND BOB BROOKS, TRUCKEE ANIMAL CONTROL.
For more information, please visit the Lake Tahoe BEAR League at *www.savebears.org*.

This mother black bear has quite a pawful of cubs to care for. In 2007, she gave birth to five healthy young in northern New Hampshire. Black bears typically have two cubs. *PHOTO: TOM SEARS, WWW.TOMSEARS.COM*

trivial but true

What do you call a group of bears? They are called a sloth, a term first used in 1452, according to the Oxford English Dictionary. The actual phrase was "A Slouthe of Beerys." The word sloth derives from the Middle English term for slow, but it is a mystery as to why early writers thought that a group of bears moved slowly. Bears have long since vanished from Britain, thus the term only had a very brief usage before going into a two-century-long dormancy, until English reached the New World. It's actually a rare sight to see a group of bears together. However, where food is plentiful, like at a salmon stream, you will often see a sloth of bears.

Five-month-old black bear sisters wrestle and play (Whistler Mountain, BC, Canada). *PHOTOS: SYLVIA DOLSON*

Below: Jeanie and her daughters, Jasmine and Jenny (June 2007), residents of Whistler Mountain, BC, Canada. Unfortunately, Jenny was killed in a vehicle collision when she was only 8 months old and Jasmine was relocated as a yearling. *PHOTO: IRENE SHEPPARD*

Learn more about Jeanie at www.bearsmart.com/Jeanie.html

These black bear cubs-of-the-year are about 5 months old (Whistler Mountain, BC, Canada). *TOP PHOTO: SYLVIA DOLSON; BOTTOM PHOTO: IRENE SHEPPARD*

A young black bear at the Wildlife Research Institute (Ely, Minnesota). *PHOTO: SYLVIA DOLSON*

Storing trash and recycling in the back of a truck, or in any vehicle, is not a good idea.
TOP PHOTO: RAINE BROOKSBANK; BOTTOM PHOTO: STEVE JOHNSON SCOTT

Black bear at Hymers, Ontario, Canada. *PHOTO: DOROTHY HAYS*

A young black bear at the Wildlife Research Institute (Ely, Minnesota).
PHOTO: SYLVIA DOLSON

Hummingbird feeders are just as attractive to bears as birdseed feeders (black bear at Mission, BC, Canada). *PHOTO: IRENE SHEPPARD*

Above: A three-year-old male black bear investigates the ski hill equipment on Blackcomb Mountain, BC, Canada. *PHOTO: SYLVIA DOLSON*
Below: Billie, a border collie cross, puts the run on a black bear at the Whistler Golf Course, Canada. *PHOTO: IRENE SHEPPARD*

Black bear cubs hurry to catch up with their mother (Whistler Mountain, BC, Canada). *PHOTO: IRENE SHEPPARD*

Out on a limb at the Wildlife Research Institute (black bear cub; Ely, Minnesota). *PHOTO: SYLVIA DOLSON*

A polar bear sniffs the wind for scent (Churchill, Manitoba, Canada).
PHOTO: SYLVIA DOLSON

trivial but true

A Polar Bear's Fur Is Not White Each hair shaft on the polar bear is pigment-free and transparent with a hollow core. They look white because the hollow core scatters and reflects visible light, much like ice and snow does. Polar bears' thick fur includes a dense undercoat topped by guard hairs of various lengths. Their insulating fur and thick blubber layer keep the bears so cozy that they experience almost no heat loss. In fact, the insulation is so effective that adult males quickly overheat when they run. *[www.polarbears international.org]*

Bears are often captured in live traps for management action. Sometimes they are relocated and other times they are killed. This little black bear cub lived to see another day (Vail, Colorado). *PHOTO: RYAN MILLBERN*

A polar bear family rests on the shore of Hudson Bay, Manitoba, Canada.
PHOTO: DAVID KRUGHOFF, WWW.PHOTOARTCANADA.COM

A resourceful black bear at Long Lake, Ontario, Canada. *PHOTOS: ERIK KALVIAINEN*

Named "Alpine," this male black bear was radio-collared for research purposes in Whistler, BC, Canada.
PHOTO: NICOLA BRABYN

VISITOR PARKING ONLY

Voytek, the Soldier-Bear

By Ryszard Antolak, *Persian Journal*, August 2005
(Condensed version; reprinted with permission)

After the Battle of Monte Cassino, one of the fiercest and bloodiest conflicts of the Second World War, many accounts emerged of the bravery and heroism of the soldiers. But perhaps the strangest story of all was of an Iranian brown bear who served alongside the Allied soldiers in the worst heat of the battle. Despite the incessant bombardment and constant gunfire, the bear carried vital supplies of ammunition and food to his fellow soldiers fighting on the mountainside. Many observers who witnessed his remarkable actions doubted the reality of what they were seeing. But the story is no legend.

At the time of his death in 1964, he was the most famous bear in the world, visited by countless celebrities and adored by the international press. Books and articles were written about him, statues and plaques commemorated his actions. To the men of the 22nd Transport Company (Artillery Supply) however, he was merely Voytek *[also spelled Woytek]*, a remarkable fellow soldier and their beloved comrade.

He was born in the mountains of Hamadan, in one of the many caves to be found in that dusty mountainous area. At the age of eight weeks his mother was killed by a group of hunters, but he was rescued by a young Iranian boy who thrust him into a hempen sack and set off with him homeward along a narrow dusty path.

Iran at that time was going through one of the unhappier periods of her history. Occupied by the Russians and the British, her relations with the soldiers of those two countries were understandably tense and strained. In April 1942, however, Iran opened her arms to receive hundreds of thousands of Polish citizens who had been released from the Soviet labour camps of Siberia and Kazakhstan. Most of the civilians (women and children) were destined to remain as guests of Iran for up to three years. But the able-bodied men were almost immediately sent westwards to join the Polish forces in Lebanon. A long stream of covered trucks left Anzali daily carrying the future soldiers along the narrow twisted roads to the borders of Iraq and beyond.

It was on one of the narrow mountain roads somewhere between Hamadan and Kangavar that the trucks were brought to an abrupt halt by the sight of a small Iranian boy carrying a bulky sack. He looked tired and hungry, so the men offered him a billy-can of meat. And as he ate, they gasped in astonishment as the sack beside him began to move and the head of a honey-colored bear cub emerged sleepily into the sunlight.

Although none of the men could understand Farsi, the boy was able to indicate by his actions that he had found the bear cub whimpering outside one of the caves, its mother having been shot by a hunter. The orphaned cub was in poor condition and it was almost certain he would not survive the day. One of the men, therefore, offered to buy the orphaned cub for a few toumans. Someone else fumbled for a bar of chocolate and a tin of corned beef to give the boy. Another took from his pocket an army pen-knife that opened up like a flower. The boy smiled, pocketed the offerings and disappeared forever from their lives.

A feeding bottle had to be hastily improvised from an empty bottle of vodka into which a handkerchief had been stuffed to serve as a teat. They filled it with condensed milk, diluted it with a little water, and gave it to the little bear to drink. When he had finished it, he crept up close to one of the soldiers for warmth and fell asleep on his chest. The soldier's name was Piotr (Peter) and he became forever afterward the bear's closest and most enduring friend.

The cub clung desperately to his substitute mother all through the tortured journey across Persia, Iraq and Jordan. Sometimes the man would lock the bear in the warmth of his greatcoat so that it became part of him. In the evenings, as he sat with the other men around the fire telling tales late into the night, the bear cub would be rocked to sleep in the sound of Piotr's immense laughter. In time, the orphan lost himself in the lives of these strangers and entangled himself completely in the rhythms and cadences of their speech. From that time onwards he became wholly theirs: body, will and soul.

In this way, Voytek the Iranian brown bear from Hamadan entered the lives of the soldiers of the Second Polish Army Corps, transforming all their destinies.

In the months that followed, he won over the hearts of all who met him. The soldiers, who had all endured the horrors and hardships of Siberia, needed something in their lives to love, and the presence of Voytek was a wonderful tonic for their morale. Despite his brute strength, which grew day by day, he was always an amiable and gentle giant. The soldiers treated him from the start as one of their own company and never as a pet. They shared their food with him, allowed him to sleep in their tents at night and included him in all their activities. If the unit was ordered to march out, he would march with them on two legs like a soldier. When they were being transported to some distant location, he would ride in the front seat of the jeeps (or transport wagons) to the great amazement of passers-by. More than anything, however, he loved to wrestle with the soldiers, taking on three or four of them at a time. Sometimes he was even gracious enough to allow them

Voytek with a soldier of the Polish 2nd Army Corps.

the courtesy of winning. Over the next few years, he went with them wherever they were posted throughout the Middle East. He grew to be almost six feet tall and weighed 500 pounds.

In early 1944, the men of Voytek's unit were ordered to embark for Italy to join the Allied advance on Rome. The British authorities gave strict instructions that no animals were to accompany them. The Poles therefore enrolled Voytek into the army as a rank-and-file member of their company and duly waved the relevant papers in front of the British officers on the dockside at Alexandria. Faced with such impeccable credentials, the British shrugged their shoulders and waved the bear aboard. In this way, Voytek the Iranian bear became an enlisted soldier in the Polish 2nd Army Corps.

Monte Cassino was the strategic key to the Allied advance on Rome. Three bloody attempts by the British, Americans, Indians, French and New Zealanders to dislodge the enemy from the famous hill-top monastery had failed. In April 1944, the Polish forces were sent in. It was one of the bloodiest battles of the war. Much of the fighting was at close quarters.

During the most crucial phase of the battle, when pockets of men desperately in need of supplies were cut off on the mountainside, Voytek, who all this time had been watching his comrades frantically loading heavy boxes of ammunition, came over to the trucks, stood on his hind legs in front of the supervising officer and stretched out his paws toward him. It was as if he was saying: I can do this; let me help you. The officer handed the animal the heavy box and watched in wonder as Voytek loaded it onto the truck. Backwards and forwards he continued, time and time again, effortlessly carrying heavy shells, artillery boxes and food sacks from truck to truck, from one waiting man to another. The deafening noise of the explosions and gunfire did not seem to worry him; he never dropped a single one. And still he went on repeatedly, all day and every day until the monastery was finally taken. One of the soldiers happened to sketch a picture of Voytek carrying a large artillery shell in his arms, and this image became the symbol of the 22nd Artillery Transport, worn proudly on the sleeves of their uniforms ever afterwards and emblazoned on all the unit's vehicles.

Now famous, he completed his tour of duty in Italy and when the war was over, he sailed with the Polish Army to exile in Scotland. Here, once again, he found himself a celebrity. In Glasgow, people lined the streets in thousands to catch sight of the famous soldier-bear marching upright in step with his comrades.

Voytek's last days, however, were steeped in sadness. In 1947, the Polish army in Scotland was demobilized and a home had to be found for him to live out his retirement.

Although he was world-famous, the bear of Monte Cassino was forced to spent his last years behind bars in Edinburgh's Zoological gardens. Artists came to sketch him and sculptors to make statues of him. Sometimes his old army friends arrived to visit him, leaping over the barriers to wrestle and play with him in the bear enclosure (to the utter horror of all the visitors and zoo officials). But he did not take well to captivity, and as the years passed, he increasingly preferred to stay indoors, refusing to meet anyone.

I was lucky enough to see him just before his death in 1963. He was sitting at the back of his large enclosure, silent and immobile. It was said that he was sulking, angry at being abandoned by those he had loved. Others said he was merely showing the symptoms of old age. None of the shouts from his assembled visitors seemed to catch his attention. But when I called out to him in Polish, something seemed to stir in him at last, and he turned his head towards me as if in recognition.

He died in Edinburgh at the age of 22 on November 15, 1963. A plaque was erected in his memory by the zoo authorities. Statues of him were placed in the Imperial War Museum in London and in the Canadian War Museum in Ottawa. But although he had entered the pages of military history, the Iranian soldier-bear of Monte Cassino would have preferred to remain in the company of the soldiers with whom he had shared five years of war and countless memories of devoted companionship. ~

Aboriginal Connections

The bear held a special place in the cultures of North America's indigenous peoples. Depending on the culture, the bear was revered as a healer and a teacher, a protector and a guardian, even a spirit helper. Many cultures also recognized the bear's fearsome power and potential for aggression, even invoking it to protect warriors before they went off to battle their enemies.

Some cultures thought bears were gods sent to earth to make men humble, others thought bears were intermediaries between humans and the Creator. Still others believed that humans, at least the more exalted leaders and hunters among them, were the descendants of a bear-human union that is celebrated in several related myths and legends.

According to the Nuxalk people of the Bella Coola area (British Columbia, Canada), when the Creator first made humans, they were shown a lodge with four robes hanging in it: an eagle, a killer whale, a raven, and a bear. Each person was asked to choose a robe to wear while descending to earth. Inside the animal robes, humans took on that animal's form for their journey. When they arrived, they could shape shift back and forth between animal and human forms, but eventually they lost their ability to transform and remained human. It is these people who eventually settled their clans, of which the bear was one of the most powerful.

The Haida version of the Bear Mother story suggests that a young Indian woman was kidnapped by two Bear People dressed in bear robes. She became the Chief's son's wife and bore him twin sons who were half bear, half human. The twins returned to their tribe and became great hunters. When their mother died, they donned their robes and returned to live with the Bear People. *(See next page for the complete story.)*

Native bear stories reflect the intimate relationship aboriginal people had with nature. People developed special connections to the land and its plants and animals, to the sky and to the elements. Central among these were the relationships they had with the animals that provided their food and other material needs.

Animals, however, were more than just sources of food or shelter. Animals aided aboriginal peoples in their everyday lives and appeared in their dreams and meditations. Each animal taught native peoples a different lesson. In the West, there were buffalo lessons and elk lessons. You could learn from the beaver and from the wolf. If you were very special, you could aspire to the power of the bear.

While it is difficult for many of us to completely understand the aboriginal peoples' spiritual connection with the bear, we can begin to learn from their unique kinship with bears if we listen carefully to their teachings. In essence, the bear becomes a symbol of our intimate and inextricable relationship with nature—that we are as much animal as the bear is, depending on each other for our survival.

Early white men's concept of the bear was fundamentally different, of course. There is no better place to look than the early Europeans' scientific name for the grizzly bear: *Ursus horribilis*, or *terrible bear*. But to indigenous peoples, they were not the terrible creatures we've been taught to fear.

"Only to the white man was nature a wilderness and only to him was the land 'infested' with 'wild' animals and 'savage' people," said Chief Luther Standing Bear of the Oglala Sioux. "To us it was tame. Earth was bountiful and we were surrounded with the blessings of the Great Mystery."

As David Rockwell indicates in *Giving Voice to Bear*, bears and aboriginal people have been sharing habitat for a very long time. For thousands of years they walked the same trails, drank and fished out of the same streams, and harvested the same roots, berries, and seeds. A great mutual respect developed between native people and bears—especially grizzlies. (The Blackfeet referred to the grizzly as *nitakyaio*, or *Real Bear*, to differentiate it from the black bear, which they called *kyaio*.)

People in many aboriginal cultures continue to share a belief that bears possess wisdom and power; few other animals have been so revered and honored with as much ritual attention. Hunting customs, ceremonial feasts, the wearing of bear hides and costumes, and the depiction of bears in art, song, story and dance signify the bear's importance to North America's original inhabitants.

The Mother of All Bear Stories

The Bear Mother Story is the great grandmother of all bear myths, the one that lies at the foundation of all Native relationships with the Great Bear. It goes something like this:

Two Bear People dressed in bear robes kidnapped a young Indian girl who was out picking berries. She should have been singing to keep the bears away, but instead she was laughing and carrying on. The bears, god-like, thought she was mocking them, so they took her away to their lodge. All of the Bear People inside also wore bear robes. Grandmother mouse ran up to the girl and told her she had been taken into the bear den and was to become one of them. She was frightened. One of the young bears, the son of a chief, came up to her and said, "You will live if you become my wife. Otherwise you will die."

Being practical, she chose to become this Bear Person's wife. She tended the fire of the dark house. She noticed that whenever any of the people left, they put on their bear robe and so became like the animal. In the winter she became pregnant. She gave birth to twins, which were half human and half bear. These became the Bear Sons.

One day her brothers came looking for her, and the Bear Wife knew she must reveal her presence. So she did. On hearing the news, the Bear Husband knew that he would die, but before he was killed by the woman's brothers, he taught her and their Bear Sons the songs that the hunters must use over his dead body to ensure their good luck. He willed his skin to her father, who was a tribal chief. The young men then killed the bear, smoking him out of the cave and spearing him. They spared the two children/cubs and took them and their Bear Mother back to her people.

When they arrived, the Bear Sons removed their bear robes and became great (human) hunters. They guided their kinsmen to bear dens in the mountains and showed them how to set snares, and they instructed the people in singing the ritual songs. Many years later, when their Bear Mother died, they put on their coats again and went back to live with the Bear People, but the tribe continued to have good fortune with their hunting. ~

The Bear Totem

Many people believe that each of us have animal totems guiding, teaching and protecting us. These totems are forces of nature we can access to guide us along our personal path of self discovery and they connect us to the spirit world. Native peoples believe totems bring teachings from the Animal Kingdom for the Two-Leggeds.

Each animal has its own special power and message, for each animal has a powerful spirit and an inherent skill. Animal spirits choose a person to be a companion and friend to, not the other way around. We usually know these animals by instinct because we are especially attracted to them throughout our lives. You can have several animal guides: some you are born with, some are permanent and never leave us. But sometimes an animal guide will come into your life for a short period of time and then be replaced by another depending on the journey or direction you are headed toward. Your totem guides will instruct and protect you as you learn how to navigate through your spiritual and physical life.

Totems can be a mammal, bird or reptile. Bears, which represent only one of the animal totems, are honored and respected by spiritualists the world over. Bears are known to impart pure and right wisdom and are therefore trusted advisors in the spiritual world. The Bear possesses many animal virtues that are powerful

did you know?

Naming the Bear Many native tribes consider the bear too sacred to call by name and instead give the bear synonymic titles, such as...

- Big Hairy One
- Honey-Eater
- Blue-Tail
- Snub Nose
- Short Tail
- Black Food
- Big-Great-Food
- Angry One
- Sticky Mouth

- Coat the Color of Night
- Broad-Foot
- The Old One
- Master of the West
- The Dog of God
- Cousin
- Grandmother
- Honey Paws
- Grandfather

[Source: *GRRRRR, A Collection of Poems about Bears*, edited by CB Follett]

and valuable and which any person would be wise to emulate or divine. One who has the power of the Bear will possess balance, harmony and strength.

Meditating and working with the Bear will awaken the power of the unconscious to help you to go within your soul's den—your inner sanctum—to find answers. The power of the Bear totem is the power of introspection; to turn inward for guidance. The Bear teaches us that a period of reflection and time to digest is necessary in order to grow and be reborn. Just as the bear hibernates during the winter, people with a Bear totem will be quieter during the winter months. But they must awaken in the spring and seek whatever opportunities are around them.

When you have a Bear totem, you are being guided to a leadership role. There is a time for playfulness and a time to be assertive. You must be fearless in defending your beliefs and have the courage to do what is right. The Bear teaches us strength in the face of adversity and how to bring dreams into concrete reality. The Bear also encourages you to exercise your abilities as a natural healer.

The Bear in Native American Horoscope/Zodiac

Native American astrology is a group of systems, traditions and beliefs based on twelve animal guides that represent the zodiac. These animals, or birth totems, help guide and teach life lessons to younger generations. The Bear is one among the animal representatives within the Native American zodiac; guiding people born from August 22nd to September 21st.

In many tribes, Bears are recognized as the head of the animals due to their strong and steadfast nature. People born under this animal will defend those they care about. Bear people are considerate, independent and hardworking. They adapt well to new situations and value tradition over technology.

Pragmatic and methodical, the Bear is the one to call when the voice of reason is needed. The Bear's practicality and levelheadedness makes him/her an excellent business partner. The Bear is also gifted with an enormous heart and a penchant for generosity. The Bear tends to be very modest and a bit shy.

The Bear has a capacity for patience and temperance, which makes him/her an excellent teacher and mentor. Left to his/her own devices, the Bear can be hypocritical, prudish and finicky. Those born under this sign should try to cultivate optimism and tolerance while avoiding skepticism, faultfinding and procrastination.

Native American Animal Signs

Bear
August 22 to September 21
*considerate, independent,
hardworking*

Wolf
February 19 to March 20
*artistic, gentle, sympathetic,
generous*

Raven
September 22 to October 22
*tolerant, good-natured, charming,
friendly*

Hawk
March 21 to April 19
*vehement and powerful,
spontaneous*

Snake
October 23 to November 22
*mysterious, ambitious, determined,
intensive, impulsive*

Beaver
April 20 to May 20
*methodical, inventive, headstrong,
shows perseverance*

Owl
November 23 to December 21
*adventurous, independent,
warmhearted and jovial*

Elk
May 21 to June 20
*moody, obliging, communicative,
fast and awake*

Goose
December 22 to January 19
*serious, composed, reliable,
hardworking*

Woodpecker
June 21 to July 21
*sympathetic, sensitive, emotional,
protecting*

Otter
January 20 to February 18
*independent, dynamic, friendly,
unconventional*

Salmon
July 22 to August 21
*enthusiastic, self-confident, proud,
full of energy*

Bruin Dreams

Sometimes bears come to us in our dreams. They represent calm, stoic strength. Bears also indicate a time of introspection, reflection and self-observation. They symbolize the cycle of life and death and renewal.

When we cross paths with the Bear in our dreams, we should set aside time to envelope ourselves in solitude and silence with a goal for rebirth and self-understanding.

If you dream of a bear sleeping or hibernating, this is a message to do a little soul searching before you present an idea to the world. If a bear is chasing you, this means you are avoiding a big issue in your life, and it is time to deal with it. If the bear is standing up, this is a sign you need to defend your beliefs.

A bear showing up in your dreams is also a symbol for play; that you need to relax and allow for some creativity in your life. The more we allow ourselves to loosen up and have fun, the more our lives begin to take on a lighter, livelier perspective. ～

did you know?

Dream Lodge Many tribes believe the Bear is the keeper of the dreamtime, and stores the teachings of dreams until the dreamer wakes up to them. They have called this space of inner-knowing the Dream Lodge, where the death of the illusion of physical reality overlays the expansiveness of eternity. It is in the Dream Lodge that our ancestors sit in Council and advise us regarding alternative pathways that lead to our goals.

Bear Clan

By Eloise Charet-Calles

My name is Eloise Charet-Calles, Bear Clan of Turtle-Island [Canada]. I have lived in the Kootenays for twenty years, often raising my children alone in the wilderness. We learned to live with our animals and respect their need for food and habitat.

I am a weaver and medicine woman. I forage for food and herbs in nature. Observing what animals eat is an important teaching. You never take from nature without asking and offering a prayer of gratitude. One learns to connect with the spirit of living things rather than their form. Bear spirit is very powerful and we must treat these animals as our relatives.

I am a grandmother and mother of the Bear Clan. It is my duty to see to the source of life and the health of the next generations of all life forms. I spent two months in jail, fasting for our watershed doomed to be clearcut. I have blocked many roads—from herbicide spraying, cutting old growth forests, and the destruction of our water. In 1998, I walked across Canada for water and what I witnessed frightened me—the loss of our precious resources and an abundance of cancer, especially on the reserves.

Bear Temptations

My four children and I were living in an old miner's cabin on Red Mountain, near Silverton, British Columbia. Sitting inside by a large window while reading our local *Valley Voice* newspaper, I heard quite a commotion. I told my daughter Emma to quiet down. She replied that she wasn't making any noise.

Putting the paper down and looking up I saw a two-year-old brown bear going through the cooler I had placed on the back porch. He was holding the lid up with one hand and with the other going through the assortment of cheese I bought recently. He was sniffing each one with the nose of a connoisseur.

First I was in shock and then I was mad. "No, not the Gouda!" He looked at me with the bag of cheese in his mouth and a smile that meant: "Yes, the Gouda!" Closing the cooler, he took off for the woods. I grabbed the broom (my feminine weapon) and chased him up the hill but alas, to no avail. In the end all I got was a red face and the wrapper with a red Gouda label.

We would see the bear almost everyday somewhere around, chewing on clover or other blossoms and sometimes in the compost. We were careful because we knew he was young and hungry.

In the fall, I was given two gallons of brandy to make tinctures. I left it on the front porch to keep cool. One night, our teenage bear sunk his teeth into the plastic container and got drunk. The next morning, I walked around to check and sure enough, there he was snoring, flat out in the garden, sleeping off his hangover for two days.

The next year, we lived in the small town of Silverton and it was a big bear year in town because there were no berries. Every day we had a mom and cub sleeping in our old growth trees, perched on a group of branches just like a hammock. Four to eight bears came through our yard every day. We would call our neighbors to keep them informed if a group was coming their way.

Late one night, my eldest son Nicholas heard a commotion outside. Rising quickly from his bed in his underwear, he went to check it out. Opening the door and walking onto the porch, he noticed a huge bear in the yard. Mesmerized by its size, he stood fascinated for what seemed like a very long time.

Suddenly, he heard something chewing right beside him. At the same moment he realized what that fuzzy, furry, warm feeling was on the side of his leg. He looked down and there was a large bear sitting, eating a pear from a box, watching the intruder as well. Nicholas let out a scream and ran for the door. The bear yelped and ran the other way, jumping off the veranda.

We were some of the few people who didn't have a dog. One time I heard a dog barking ferociously in our yard. Going outside I found a large male bear up in the tree crying. He was really scared. I took the dog back to the neighbors and upon my return the bear came down and gave me a look of gratitude with a high pitch sound I will never forget.

A young woman once told me she had found some mild hallucinogenic mushrooms and made little chocolate squares out of them. She put them on the open windowsill to cool off and went out. Upon returning she saw a cinnamon bear lying out in the field and discovered half her chocolates were gone. She was worried and stayed awake most of the night. The next afternoon, she heard a noise by the window and there was the same cinnamon bear with two buddies.

Last summer, in New Denver where I presently live, I was stopping big trucks coming down the road to allow two little crying twin bears to join their mother on the other side of the highway. The whole village was patient with them as they visited various yards to enjoy the ripening fruit.

Unfortunately the bears entered the village campground and all five bears—two mothers and three cubs—were shot the next morning.

We live in a society that does not honor the bears, destroys their habitat and shoots moms and babes. The gun is a faster solution than mediation and compassion. We must learn to be part of the web of life rather than dominate or manage nature. It is a consciousness we must achieve in order to bring about PEACE in our lifetime and leave a living legacy for future generations. ~

PHOTO: SYLVIA DOLSON

FAMOUS BEARS

Smokey the Bear

Smokey the Bear was best known for his stern warning to Americans: "Remember! Only you can prevent forest fires." The deep-voiced black bear in the ranger hat was created in 1944 as part of a campaign to prevent human carelessness from destroying commercially valuable timber resources. Smokey is still the poster bear for forest fire prevention in the United States—the longest running public service campaign in history.

In 1950, firefighters in New Mexico's Lincoln National Forest found an abandoned bear cub. A photograph of the tiny cub licking a little girl's face appeared in newspapers throughout the U.S., and the cub was quickly christened Smokey after "Smokey" Joe Martin, a legendary New York City fire chief. Smokey, the living symbol of the poster bear, grew old and died in the National Zoo in Washington, D.C. He lies buried beneath a plaque in Capitan, New Mexico, one of the few black bears in history to receive a funeral. Thousands of people still visit his grave every year.

Smokey, the poster bear, continues to live on, warning new generations of campers to keep forests safe from fire. Real black bears actually prefer burned areas to mature forests or clearcuts because of the abundance of new growth. ~

trivial but true

What was Smokey the Bear's original name? Hotfoot Teddy.

How Much Do You Know About Smokey?

- **What kind of bear?** American black bear
- **Adult Weight?** 300-plus pounds Smokey has black bear relatives who weigh over 800 pounds. Some of his grizzly cousins weigh almost a ton!
- **His weight at birth?** Less than a pound.
- **Favorite Clothes?** Smokey the Bear hat, blue jeans and belt. Smokey is most frequently seen standing upright with a shovel in hand.
- **Favorite Saying?** "Remember! Only you can prevent forest fires."
- **Favorite Foods?** Forest takeout—nuts, ants, salmon, grasses, roots and berries.
- **Favorite Winter Activity?** Heavy sleep accompanied by slow heart rate. Smokey will awake if the weather is warm or he is disturbed. He eats a year's worth of food in 6–8 months so he has a layer of fat that keeps him going through the denning period.
- **What Smokey Needs?** Your help! Smokey and his forest pals need you to be careful, not careless—especially with cigarette butts and camp fires. Smokey, the poster bear, is a good public servant in warning campers to keep the forests safe from fire.

More fun information can be found at: www.smokeybear.com

trivial but true

How did highway patrol officers get nicknamed "Smokey"?
Smokey wears a hat similar to one worn by many U.S. state police officers, giving rise to the CB slang "bear" or Smokey.

Bears in Our Language

Bears have not just found their way into our hearts and imaginations, but into our everyday language and daily lives. The
constellations of Ursa Major and Ursa Minor are not the only
things named for bears...

Bearly a Figure of Speech

The physical attributes and behaviors of bears are commonly
used in figures of speech.

In the stock market, a *bear market* is a period of declining
prices. Pessimistic forecasting or negative activity is said to be
bearish (due to the stereotypical posture of bears looking down-
wards), and one who expresses bearish sentiment is a *bear*. Its
opposite is a bull market, and bullish sentiment from bulls.

A *bear* is also an investor who sells commodities, securities,
or futures in anticipation of a fall in prices. Bears specifically look
for over-priced securities to sell short.

Try like a bear means you are trying your hardest to catch the

trivial but true

Bears Get Minted On February 19, 1996, the Canadian two-dollar
bill was replaced with the two-dollar bimetallic coin, commonly
known as a "Twoonie" or "Toonie." The coin's reverse side depicts
a polar bear standing on an ice floe.

attention of a certain lady. The harder you try, the better the bear you are.

Bear may also refer to a problem that is very difficult to solve: *that was a bear of a problem.*

A *bear hug* is typically a tight hug that involves wrapping your arms around another person, often leaving their arms immobile.

If you are *hungry as a bear*, it means that you are really hungry. The saying probably originated as a result of bears eating twenty hours a day during the fall to pack on the pounds for winter hibernation.

"There is a bear in the woods" was the opening line of an effective political television commercial formally titled "Bear" or "If There Is a Bear." The ad was part of the 1984 U.S. presidential campaign of Republican Party candidate Ronald Reagan. It featured a brown bear wandering through a forest accompanied by ominous narration that suggested the Soviet Union (traditionally symbolized by a bear) was a serious threat to global stability, which Ronald Reagan recognized and was better prepared to deal with than his opponent. Then the image shifted to a hunter facing the bear; the ad ended with a picture of Reagan and the tagline:

trivial but true

What state animal is long gone? The California grizzly bear. It even appears on their state flag today as a symbol of great strength. Ironically, all grizzlies were eradicated from the state by 1924. The last known California grizzly was a bear named Monarch. He was captured by William Randolph Hearst and gifted to the City of San Francisco, where he was housed in a special enclosure in Golden Gate Park. After his death he was stuffed and mounted for display at the California Academy of Science. In 1955, this stuffed bear served as the model for the current specifications for the California state flag.

"President Reagan: Prepared for Peace." *There is a bear in the woods* continues to be a popular phrase to invoke when a potential problem looms on the horizon, especially in political circles.

In the old western United States and former Dakota Territory, the phrase, *you ain't just a bear trackin,* used to mean "you ain't lying" or "that's for sure" or "you're not just blow'n smoke." The expression "bear tracking" evolved as a result of the experience pioneer hunters and mountainmen had when tracking bear. Bears often lay down false tracks and are notorious for doubling back. Figuratively speaking, then, if you are not following bear tracks, you are not following false trails or leads in your thoughts, words or deeds.

trivial but true

What word sounds the same as "bear," but has a different meaning? Bare

What is the origin of "bruin"? It is a folk name for bear, related to the Old English "brun," especially brown bears.

Bear: In Name Only

The proper names of cities such as Bern, Berlin and Bergin, as well as personal names such as Bernard, Bertha, Gilbert, Herbert, and Robert derive from "bear."

If your name is Robert, you can evoke the French pronunciation of the name, *Ro-bear,* which probably means something like "he who rolls around with bears," "he who is sympathetic to old honey-paws" or "a porky-SOB-who-hikes-alone-and-is-good-bear-bait."

In Scandinavia (particularly in Sweden) the word for bear, Björn (pronounced Bee-uhh-rn) or Bjorn, is a relatively common first name for males. The use of this name most likely stems from prehistoric times and has been found mentioned in several rune-stone inscriptions. The name was also used by J.R.R. Tolkien in his book *The Hobbit,* where a bear-like character is named Beorn.

Are You Multi-Bear Lingual?

The bear as named in other languages:

Algonquin	Muk-Wah
Chinese (中文)	熊 (xióng)
Czech (Česky)	Medvěd
Danish (dansk)	Bjørne
Dutch (Nederlands)	Beer
Filipino (Tagalog)	Oso
Finnish (suomi)	Karhu
French (Français)	Ours
German (Deutsch)	Bär
Greek (Ελληνικά)	Αρκούδα (arkutha)
Hindi (हिन्दी)	भालू (bhalu)
Hungarian (magyar)	Medve
Icelandic (Íslenska)	Björn
Italian (Italiano)	Orso
Japanese (日本語)	クマ (kuma)
Latin (latina)	Ursus
Malay (bahasa Melayu)	Beruang
Navajo	Shash
Norwegian (Norsk)	Bjørn
Polish (polski)	Niedźwiedź
Portuguese (Português)	Urso
Romanian (Română)	Urs
Russian (Русский язык)	медведь (medved')
Slovenian (Slovenščina)	Medved
Spanish (Español)	Oso
Swedish (svenska)	Björn
Turkish (Türkçe)	Ayı
Welsh (Cymraeg)	Arth

The female first name Ursula, originally derived from a Christian saint's name and common in English- and German-speaking countries, means *Little She-Bear* (dimunitive of Latin Ursa). In Switzerland, the male first name, Urs, is especially popular.

In Russian and other Slavic languages, the word for bear, Medved, and derivatives such as Medvedev, are common surnames.

In East European Jewish communities, the Yiddish name, Ber, has been a common first name for men since the eighteenth century, and was the name of several prominent Rabbis. Ber is still in use among Orthodox Jewish communities in Israel, the United States and other countries.

With the transition from Yiddish to Hebrew under the influence of Zionism, the Hebrew word for bear, Dov, was taken up in contemporary Israel and is at present one of the commonly used male first names in that country.

What's In a Name?

The name *panda* originates with a Himalayan language, possibly Nepali, and was originally applied to the red panda.

In Chinese, the name for the giant panda literally translates to *large bear cat*, or just *bear cat*. And in Taiwan, the modern name for panda is *cat bear*. There are two explanations for the origin of this name. Physiologically, the eyes of most other bear species have round pupils, but the giant pandas' pupils are vertical slits like cats' eyes. These unusual eyes, combined with its ability to effortlessly scale trees, may be what inspired the Chinese to call the panda the *bear cat*.

On the other hand, some researchers believe that the name *bear cat* originally belonged to the red panda, which also lives on bamboo in China and are actually cat-size. When Himalayan peoples first saw the giant panda, they named it *large bear cat,* due to the similarities in behaviors and habitat.

However, locals from different provinces use different names such as spotted bear and bamboo bear for the giant panda. Prior to 1900, the giant panda was known as mottled bear (*Ailuropus melanoleucus*) or particolored bear.

did you know?

The Malayan sun bear is often called the "dog bear" because of its small stature, but its Malay and Indonesian name is Beruang Madu ("Honey Bear").

What's Named after a Bear, but Looks Like a Raccoon?

It's the red panda, but it's neither a bear or a raccoon. The red panda has its own independent family in the scientific classification system, called *Ailuridae*, whereas the bear is classified as an *Ursidae*. The taxonomic classification of both the red panda and giant panda has actually been under debate for many decades, as both species share characteristics of bears and raccoons.

While the red panda and giant panda share the same name, they are only very distantly related by remote common ancestry from the Early Tertiary Period. Its common ancestor can be traced back tens of millions of years. Fossils of the red panda have been unearthed from China in the east to Britain in the west and most recently a handful of fossils have also been discovered in North America. ~

Bear Mythologies of Scandinavia

In Scandinavia, there was a firm belief in the ability of some people to change into or assume the characteristics of bears. Our English word "berserk" comes from this legend. It was thought that if a warrior was to don a bear-skin shirt (called a bear-sark) which had been treated with oils and herbs, the warrior would gain the strength, stamina and power of the animal. These people would be driven into a frenzy in battle and were said to be capable of biting through the enemy's shields or walking through fire without injury. No matter how much of the legend is true, the thought of a group of Vikings made up as bears is sobering. *[www.bears.org]*

trivial but true

Daredevils of Niagara Falls People have been hurtling them-selves in various vessels over Niagara Falls throughout history. The first was in 1827. Some men got an old ship—the Michigan—which had been pronounced unseaworthy. For mere wantonness, they put aboard a bear, a fox, a buffalo, a dog and some geese and sent it over the falls. The bear jumped from the vessel before it reached the rapids, swam toward the shore, and was rescued by some caring bystanders. The geese went over the falls and reached the shore below alive. The dog, fox, and buffalo were not heard of nor seen again.

A Bear of a Sports Team

Alberta Golden Bears	University of Alberta
Baylor Bears	Baylor University
Black Bears	University of Maine
Brisbane Bears	Former Australian Rules Football team
California Golden Bears	University of California, Berkeley
Central Arkansas Bears	University of Central Arkansas
Chicago Bears	American football team
Missouri State Bears	Missouri State University
North Sydney Bears	Australian rugby league team
NYIT Bears	New York Institute of Technology
Bears	University of Northern Colorado
Sheffield Bears IHC	Ice hockey club of the University of Sheffield and Sheffield Hallam University, UK

Bear Mascots

A polar bear was chosen as mascot for the 1988 Winter Olympics held in Calgary, Canada. The polar bear is also the mascot of Bowdoin College. A black bear is the mascot for Baylor University where two bears are kept on campus, even though animal welfare advocates oppose the captives.

trivial but true

Which Canadian territories or provinces have a licence plate in the shape of a polar bear? Northwest Territories and Nunavut

EXPLORE CANADA'S ARCTIC
27541
NORTHWEST TERRITORIES

trivial but true

Are there bears in jail?
Yup, in Churchill, Manitoba, Canada. Officially, the building was once a morgue on a former military base, but now it's being used to keep up to twenty-three polar bears alive at a time! In the past, many polar bears were killed if they came too close to the town of Churchill. Now they're kept in the "Polar Bear Jail" during the late fall until the pack ice freezes, then released to join their brethren in Hudson Bay for the seal hunt.

trivial but true

Advertisers capitalize on the lure of bears In 1993, Coca-Cola brought polar bears into the homes of millions of people around the world in a commercial, "Northern Lights" in which polar bears drink coke and view the northern lights. There have been many polar bear spots since the 1993 debut, including one ad that shows polar bears partying with penguins at an Arctic beach party. In reality, they live on opposite poles: penguins live in the Antarctic and polar bears live in the Arctic.

Heraldry and Other Symbolic Use

The bear is a common charge (symbol) in heraldry. It represents a fierce opponent, as well as unsurpassable strength and a passion for battle. Numerous cities around the world have adopted the bear in their arms, notably the Swiss capital Bern, which takes its name from the German word for bears, *Bären*. In Switzerland, artists painted heraldic bears with bright red penises so they wouldn't be mocked for using she-bears.

The bear is a common national personification for Russia (as well as the Soviet Union) and even Germany. The brown bear is Finland's national animal. In the United States, the black bear is the state animal of Louisiana, New Mexico and West Virginia; the grizzly bear is the state animal of both Montana and California.

Arms of Dietingen,
Germany

Arms of Berlin,
Germany

Greenland
Coat of Arms

Arms of Portein,
Switzerland

Arms of Bern,
Switzerland

Goldilocks and the Three Bears

A very popular and notable children's bedtime story, *Goldilocks and the Three Bears*, finds its origins as an anonymous folk story. Different versions of the tale have been told and re-told since Brothers Grimm first published it in 1837. Even today, the story continues to grow and change, with one version even being told from the bears' perspective.

In one of the earliest accounts, the three bears were intruded upon by a female fox. Later, the she-fox became an angry old woman. It wasn't until 1894 that the story had the intruder help herself to milk and lounge around on beds belonging to the bears. Different and sometimes conflicting versions of the story appeared simultaneously. A little girl named Silver-Hair crept into one version of the story in 1856. She became Silver-Locks in 1889 and Goldilocks in 1904.

The modern tale unfolds as Goldilocks finds a house in the woods that belongs to three bears: papa bear, mama bear and baby bear. The three left their house unlocked and decided to go for a stroll in the woods while waiting for their porridge to cool. The curious little girl intrudes upon the house and the bears' belongings, sampling their porridge (the first bowl was too hot, the second bowl too cold, but baby bear's bowl was just right); sitting on their chairs (the first two were too big, but the baby bear's chair was just right); and then trying out their beds (the first was too hard, the second too soft and, of course, the third was just right) and she fell asleep in baby bear's bed. Goldilocks was still asleep when the bears returned home and scared her off. ~

Modern Day Tale of Three "Garbage" Bears

Bruin Funnies

Be Bear Aware

Wildlife Agencies often put up warnings to hikers in bear country, advising that they wear noisy little bells on their clothing so as not to startle any bears, and to carry bear spray with them in case of an encounter with a bear. They also suggest that it is a good idea to watch out for signs of bear activity, like scratches on trees and fresh droppings, and to be able to recognize the difference between a black and a grizzly bear.

So how do you tell the difference between black bear and grizzly bear droppings? Black bear droppings are smaller and contain berries and grass. Grizzly bear droppings have little bells and smell like pepper.

A Tale of Two Hikers

Joe and Bob are out in the woods hiking. All of a sudden a bear starts chasing them. They climb a tree, but the bear starts climbing up the tree after them.

Joe gets his sneakers out of his knapsack and starts putting them on.

Bob asks, "What are you doing?"

Joe says, "I figure when the bear gets too close, we'll have to jump down and make a run for it."

Bob replies, "Are you crazy? You can't outrun a bear!"

Joe says, "I don't have to outrun the bear. I only have to outrun you."

How does a black bear stop a VCR?

It just presses the "paws" button.

What are grizzly bears called when they get caught in the rain?

Drizzly bears.

How do you keep a bear from charging?

Insist that it pay cash!

Where do you find grizzly bears?

It depends on where you lost them.

What's a balanced diet for a polar bear?

A seal in each paw!

What did the polar bear cub say to its mother at mealtime?

"Ahh, no! Not SEALS again!"

Why do polar bears have fur coats?

Because the seals laughed at them when they wore parkas.

What do polar bears like to eat in the cold?

A "brrr"-"grrr"!

What did the Polar Bear say when it saw a seal on a skateboard?

"Meals on Wheels"

The Atheist and The Bear

An atheist is paddling down the river when he sees a grizzly swimming directly towards him. He begins to panic and figures he'd better pray to God.

Suddenly everything stops moving. The river stops flowing, the bear stops swimming. The clouds part, the sky opens up and God appears. "Why have you summoned me?"

"Oh God, I know I haven't been a good Christian for most of my life, but I swear that if you save me from this bear, I promise to become a devout Christian!"

God answers, "You think that you can forsake me and then conveniently decide to become a Christian in order to get yourself out of this situation? Forget it!"

The atheist pleads, "Please, Lord, can you at least make the bear into a Christian?"

"Hmmm. All right. Now that I can do!"

So the sky closes up. The river resumes flowing, but the bear keeps swimming towards the atheist. When he reaches the canoe, the bear folds his paws together in prayer, "Thank you, Lord, for this meal I am about to receive!"

Nuisance Bears

McNeil River, Alaska. *PHOTO: LARRY AUMILLER; ALASKA DEPARTMENT OF FISH AND GAME*

Where To See Bears

GRIZZLY BEARS

McNeil River State Game Sanctuary, Alaska

Arguably the world's most famous bear viewing site, McNeil River is a place where as many as seventy bears can be seen through the course of a day. You can get excellent photographs without long telephoto lenses. At the falls, bears may be as close as 30 feet, but the general distance is 75 to 200 feet. Visiting the site requires a permit from the Alaska Department of Fish and Game, and they limit the number of people at any one time to ten. Permits are granted by lottery. Applications can be downloaded online (deadline is March 1st of each year). The typical stay is about four days between June 7 and August 25. You will need to bring your own camping gear as there are no commercial facilities available other than a cook cabin. July is the best time to visit!
www.wildlife.alaska.gov

Brooks Falls, Katmai, Alaska

Brooks Falls, located in Katmai National Park, is world renowned for incredible grizzly bear viewing opportunities. During the peak of the world's largest sockeye salmon run each July, and during the return of the "spawned out" salmon in September, forty to sixty bears congregate in Brooks Camp along the Brooks River and the Naknek Lake and Brooks Lake shorelines. Rangers are on hand to provide information. There are many commercial bear viewing packages available in this location. Special viewing platforms, connected by an extensive boardwalk, offer unobstructed, up-close bear viewing—especially the one at the base of the falls. This is likely the location where most photographers get their clichéd shot of a salmon landing in the mouth of a grizzly. While there may be fewer bears in September, it is recommended over July as there also fewer mosquitoes and tourists. Although you can take a day trip to Brooks Falls, it's best to spend a few days there—between weather, flight delays, and bear jams (i.e. the bears frequently decide to take naps on the trail and you have to wait until they wake up), you may never even make it down to the actual falls. Lodging (must be reserved at least one year in advance) and camping are available. *www.nps.gov/katm*

Brooks Falls, Katmai National Park, Alaska. *PHOTO: MELISSA ACKERMAN*

Grizzly bear (above) and grizzly tracks in the mud (right) at Katmai National Park. *PHOTOS: LINDA MASTERSON*

Wolverine Creek, Alaska

Every year, as the enormous runs of sockeye salmon return to the Big River Lakes in Alaska, camera-friendly grizzly bears stroll up to the creek to fill their bellies. Only a 50-minute flight from Anchorage, this trip is great for enthusiasts with limited time or a smaller budget. All viewing is done from boats so you can get within 10 to 50 feet of the bears—great for extreme close-up shots. This is one of the few sites where you can watch black bears interact with grizzly bears. On a really lucky day, you might even see a bear hunting beaver. A word of warning though: the river is heavily used by fisherman, so it's often tough to avoid getting people or fishing gear in your pictures. Lodging available. July is the best time to go. To avoid fog delays, book an afternoon flight.

BLACK BEARS

Whistler-Blackcomb Bear and Wildlife Viewing Tours, Whistler, British Columbia, Canada

Accompany local experts as they guide you on a three-hour tour through the black bear habitat of Whistler Blackcomb Mountains in British Columbia—a diverse area of forests, interspersed with ski trails, that provides food and shelter for some fifty black bears. In a comfortable 4x4 vehicle, you will visit previously used bear dens, daybeds and feeding sites. You may even witness a playful interaction between a mother and her cubs or a mating pair. Deer, coyotes, marmots and raptors may also be seen. Extensive lodging and camping available in this resort. Best time to go is June into mid-July.

www.whistlerblackcomb.com/todo/summer/bears/index.htm

PHOTOS: SYLVIA DOLSON

Vince Shute Wildlife Sanctuary, Orr, Minnesota

The Vince Shute Wildlife Sanctuary, in the northern woods of Minnesota, is a place of wonder where people can learn about black bears by observing them in their natural habitat from an elevated viewing platform. The Sanctuary provides a unique opportunity to view and photograph the intimate world of the normally reclusive black bear. A must-stop on any vacation through the area, and worth a special trip just to visit the Sanctuary. Open from Memorial Day to Labor Day—there's always lots of bears. Lodging and camping available nearby. *www.americanbear.org*

Viewing platform at Vince Shute Wildlife Sanctuary.
PHOTO: BILL LEA, WWW.BILLLEA.COM

North American Bear Center, Ely, Minnesota

There are many interesting and educational exhibits at the Center, including a hands-on activity area for children, dozens of educational video clips showing how wild bears live around Ely, a theatre featuring the best in bear documentaries, and of course, the Bear Necessities gift shop. If you want to get up close and personal with bears in a natural forest setting, meet Minnesota's largest bear, Ted, and his friends, Honey and Lucky. *www.bear.org*

Black Bear Field Study Course, Ely, Minnesota

This is one of my absolute favorite top ten "life" experiences. Courses emphasize daily close-up observation of wild bears to learn their vocalizations, body language, social organization, ecology, and how people can better coexist with them. Participants stay at the Wildlife Research Institute, a place that black bears visit 24 hours a day during bear season. The small class size of eight people maximizes individual opportunities to participate in black bear research. Daily 45-minute discussions and slide presentations amplify the information learned directly from the

bears. The course offers an unprecedented opportunity to safely observe bears, including mothers interacting with their cubs. Dr. Lynn Rogers and Sue Mansfield are co-instructors. Courses run throughout the summer, but fill up quickly, so plan well in advance. *www.bearstudy.org*

PHOTO: SYLVIA DOLSON

did you know?

A national treasure? Pandas were widely hunted by the local people before 1949. By the late 1980s, a poacher could potentially receive the death penalty for killing a giant panda, but the financial reward for selling its pelt was so high (more than an average peasant's lifetime earnings) that not even the death penalty was a deterrent: "Even though I risked my life, it was worth it," a poacher was quoted as saying to police. "If you hadn't caught me, I would have been rich." In 1995, a Chinese farmer who shot and killed a giant panda and tried to sell its skin was sentenced to life imprisonment. Today, most people realize that the panda is a national treasure and they would rather help it than kill it.

POLAR BEARS
Churchill, Manitoba, Canada

In October, November and early December the town of Churchill becomes the polar bear capital of the world while bears congregate on the shore waiting for the pack ice to form. Although it's a bit out of the way, there are lots of amenities in Churchill to ensure your comfort, including numerous tours and accommodations. It's worth spending at least one day in a tundra buggie. One of my favorite trips is led by Dr. Charles Jonkel of the Great Bear Foundation. They run field courses combining adventure with learning. *www.greatbear.org/fieldcourses.htm*

Two polar bears play with a pile of seaweed. *PHOTO: SYLVIA DOLSON*

trivial but true

Do people make a tasty treat for a polar bear? No, they don't. Polar bears eat ringed seals because they're high in fat, not protein. Polar bears' bodies require water to urinate and flush out poisonous by-products that result from breaking down the protein. Since fresh water is hard to come by in the Arctic, polar bears need to conserve it. They will actually only eat the seal's blubber and leave the rest behind for scavengers. Luckily for the polar bear, they can get their water from the chemical reaction that breaks down the fat.

Viewing Bears Resources

Recommended Reading

Bear Viewing in Alaska: Expert Techniques for a Great Adventure by Stephen F. Stringham, Photography by Kent Fredriksson (Falcon Guides, 2007). Get the facts on making the most of your trip as well some tips on some of the less crowded bear viewing sites. Check out all of Stringham's books at *www.bear-viewing-in-alaska.info*.

Website Resources

For more information on these locations and others, visit *www.bearsmart.com/moreStuff/BearAdventures.html*

FAMOUS BEARS

Winnie the Pooh

In 1914, when Canadian Lieutenant Harry Colebourn was en route to military training in Eal Cardier, Quebec, he stopped in White River, Ontario and bought a black bear cub for $20 from a hunter who had killed its mother. The animal-loving Colebourn named the cub "Winnipeg" after his hometown in Manitoba and allowed it to sleep under his cot. Winnie, as she was later nicknamed, became a familiar sight around camp and the brigade soon adopted her as its mascot.

When Colebourn was ordered to the battlefields of France, he had to make arrangements for the little bear's care. Winnie was donated to the London Zoo, where she became a popular attraction, entertaining thousands of British children before she died at the ripe old age of 30. Among her many young fans was Christopher Robin Milne, who named his own teddy bear after "Winnie" and "Pooh"—a swan the family had met while on holiday. Later in 1926, his father, A.A. Milne, created the rather brainless, honey-loving character, Winnie the Pooh, who has enchanted generations of children ever since. ∿

trivial but true

When is Winnie the Pooh's birthday? August 21, 1921 is the day that the little stuffed bear was given to Christopher Robin Milne for his first birthday.

Take the
Bear-Smart Challenge

1. Which species of bears make their home in North America?
a. black bears
b. grizzly bears
c. polar bears
d. all of the above

2. What is a group of bears called?
a. troup
b. family
c. sloth
d. pack

3. How long can bears live?
a. up to 10 years
b. 10–15 years
c. 15–20 years
d. more than 20 years

4. How do scientists tell the age of a bear?
a. by size and weight
b. by taking a cross-section of a tooth and counting the rings
c. by counting the number of teeth
d. it is not possible to determine a bear's age

5. How many toes do bears have on each paw?
a. three
b. four
c. five
d. six

6. How many calories can a bear consume in one day?
a. 1,000
b. 5,000
c. 10,000
d. 20,000

7. **Which of the following are a threat to bears?**
a. poaching
b. hunting
c. habitat loss
d. all of the above
e. none of the above

8. **What is the bear's keenest sense?**
a. sight
b. smell
c. hearing
d. touch

9. **Why do bears raid bee hives?**
a. to get the honey
b. they are attracted by a hormone the bees release
c. to eat the larvae
d. they actually don't raid bee hives

10. **How do bears communicate with each other?**
a. body postures
b. vocalizations
c. odor signals
d. all of the above

11. **Why don't bears get lost in the woods?**
a. they have precise mental maps of their territory in their brains
b. they can sense the earth's magnetic field
c. scientists don't know why
d. bears get lost all the time

12. **Which of the following might attract a bear to your backyard?**
a. dirty barbecue grills
b. compost
c. dandelions
d. dog food
e. all of the above

13. **What is the number one cause of death to bears?**
a. old age
b. disease
c. human causes
d. infanticide

14. **Why do bears stand on their hind legs?**
a. to indicate a false charge
b. to show their size to an adversary
c. to better identify what has caught their attention
d. to display a threatening posture

Answers on page 174

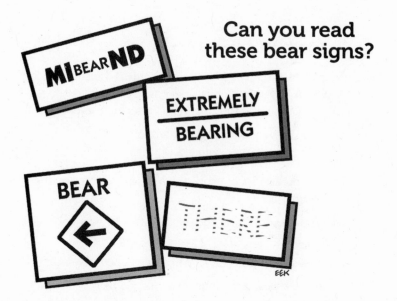

Can you read these bear signs?

MIBEAR**ND**

EXTREMELY
—
BEARING

BEAR ←

THERE

EEK

Beary Interesting Word Scramble

Unscramble the letters to learn some fun bear facts.

1. A female bear is called a WSO.
2. A male bear is call a RABO.
3. A group of bears is called a LHSOT.
4. A cub of the year is called a YCO.
5. The period of winter dormancy is called NAHBRTIENO.
6. A bear eats both plants and animals and is therefore an EIOMVONR.
7. Sounds that bears make to communicate are AVICOLNAZITOS.
8. An increase in food intake beyond the normal amount is called YGHARPHEAPI.

Answers on page 174

Test Your Voca-bear-lary!

Here's a trivia test that will allow you to scratch the surface of your vocabulary skills. This is a beary special quiz for ursophiles—all the answers contain the letters **b-e-a-r**.

1. Take into account or having remembered.

2. Hair growing on the lower part of a man's face.

3. Causing, predicting, or expecting a fall, as in prices on the stock exchange.

4 A rich sauce containing egg yolks, butter, vinegar and tarragon.

5. So unpleasant, distasteful, or painful as to be intolerable.

6. The practice of setting dogs on a chained bear.

7. A shrub native to North America and Eurasia, having small leathery leaves, white or pinkish urn-shaped flowers, and red berrylike fruits. Also called kinnikinnick.

8. Acting in a dictatorial manner, arrogant, domineering.

9. One of several funeral participants who helps carry the casket of a deceased person.

10. Also known as a bodylock, this is a grappling term used in wrestling for a clinch hold and stand-up grappling position where the arms are wrapped around the opponent, either around the opponent's chest, midsection, or thighs; some-times with one or both of the opponents arms pinned to the opponent's body.

Answers on page 174

Find and Circle These Words:

The first one is done for you.

rub	panda	dominance	mating	timid
ursus	ominivore	coexist	litter	bluff
nanulak	scent	heirarchy	tolerant	predictable
habituated	den	memory	intelligent	kermode
medved	oso	karhu	shash	beer*
bearbells	carrion	osha	conflict	sloth
berries	salmon	ants	nuts	pooh
cub	yearling	sow	boar	scat

*Beer is *Bear* in Dutch

H	A	B	I	T	U	A	T	E	D	A	D	G	B	U	R	G	E
S	C	Z	V	R	B	N	I	D	E	O	S	O	S	D	F	G	L
E	X	S	S	K	L	T	M	E	N	Q	M	A	T	I	N	G	B
F	F	U	L	B	O	S	I	R	W	S	F	I	U	I	L	P	A
H	S	A	K	I	P	U	D	T	V	D	A	D	N	A	P	O	T
N	L	F	S	E	I	R	R	E	B	W	N	Q	E	A	V	O	C
T	O	L	E	R	A	N	T	Y	K	A	L	U	N	A	N	H	I
M	T	G	J	E	W	S	C	E	N	T	B	W	T	K	C	C	D
K	H	S	A	H	S	O	R	O	D	V	B	L	R	S	E	A	E
O	X	L	H	N	O	M	L	A	S	J	E	K	O	F	G	I	R
C	B	L	F	C	O	E	X	I	S	T	E	W	T	A	C	S	P
O	U	E	M	D	X	M	C	D	U	H	R	A	K	I	J	C	O
N	B	B	E	W	N	B	N	R	O	O	N	O	I	R	R	A	C
F	D	R	D	Q	B	H	E	I	R	A	R	C	H	Y	N	E	E
L	P	A	V	W	O	S	D	A	V	G	N	I	L	R	A	E	Y
I	O	E	E	E	O	W	O	Y	R	O	M	E	M	N	O	P	E
C	I	B	D	W	R	B	P	S	H	E	R	E	T	T	I	L	S
T	U	T	T	R	T	N	E	G	I	L	L	E	T	N	I	D	D

Answers on page 174

Answers:

Page 169 - Bear Smart Challenge

1. d; 2. c; 3. d; 4. b; 5. c; 6. d; 7. d; 8. b; 9. c; 10. d;
11. c; 12. e; 13. c; 14. c

Page 171 - Reading the Signs

A. bear in mind; B. extremely over bearing; C. bear left;
D. bearly there

Page 171 - Word Scramble

1. SOW 2. BOAR 3. SLOTH 4. COY 5. HIBERNATION
6. OMNIVORE 7. VOCALIZATIONS 8. HYPERPHAGIA

Page 172 - Test Your Voca-bear-lary

1. bear in mind; 2. beard; 3. bearish; 4. Béarnaise sauce;
5. unbearable; 6. bearbaiting; 7. bearberry; 8. overbearing;
9. pallbearer; 10. bear hug

Page 173 - Word Search

Beary Special Recipes

Bear Claws

2/3 cup powdered sugar
1/2 cup almond paste
1 egg slightly beaten
dash salt
1 can (8 oz) refrigerated crescent rolls
2 - 4 tablespoons powdered sugar
2 tablespoons sliced almonds

Combine 2/3 cup powdered sugar, almond paste, 2 tablespoons beaten egg (reserve remaining egg for glaze), and salt; beat until smooth.

Unroll crescent dough to form two 13- x 4-inch rectangles. Press perforations to seal. Spread almond mixture lengthwise down center third of rectangles. Fold uncovered dough over almond mixture.

Cut each strip into 4 pieces; place on greased cookie sheet, seam side down. Brush surface with remaining egg and sprinkle with powdered sugar. On each piece, cut 4 slashes from one folded edge to center; bend dough slightly to separate slashes. Sprinkle tops with almonds.

Bake at 375°F for 12-15 minutes until golden. Makes 8 bear claws.

Blueberry Scat Cakes

1-1/2 cups unbleached flour
1-1/2 teaspoons baking soda
3/4 teaspoon baking powder
1 tablespoon brown sugar
1/4 teaspoon salt
2 eggs
1-1/2 cups plain yogurt

1/2 cup milk
zest of one orange
1/2 cup fresh orange juice
1 tablespoon butter
    or cooking oil
fresh blueberries
maple syrup

In a large bowl, combine the dry ingredients. In a separate bowl, lightly whisk the eggs. Add the liquid ingredients to the eggs and stir well to combine. Add the wet mix to the dry mix; gently folding them together. Let the batter rest for a few minutes as your griddle heats up to 350º F.

Brush the griddle with a light coat of oil or butter and use a 1/3 cup measure to ladle the batter onto the pan. Cook until small bubbles appear on the uncooked surface and the edges begin to dry. Flip the cakes over and cook a few minutes more. Serve immediately with fresh blueberries and maple syrup. Serves 2 -3.

Cinnamon Bear Muffins

1/3 cup vegetable oil
1/3 cup milk
1 teaspoon vanilla
1 or 2 eggs
2/3 cup applesauce

1/2 cup brown sugar
2 cups whole-wheat flour
1/4 teaspoon cinnamon
2 teaspoons baking powder
1/4 teaspoon salt

In a small bowl, mix all wet ingredients. In a large bowl, combine all dry ingredients. Add wet mixture to dry ingredients and stir just until blended. Fill muffin cups. Bake at 350º F for 20–25 minutes. Makes 12 large muffins.

Bear Drop Cookies

1 cup butter
1 cup peanut butter
1 cup white sugar
1 cup brown sugar
1 cup flour
1 cup quick cooking oats

3 teaspoons baking soda
3 eggs
1 cup coconut
1 cup raisins
1 cup chopped nuts
1 cup chocolate chips

Mix together all ingredients. Drop heaping teaspoonfuls of batter onto oiled cookie sheet, leaving sufficient space between drops. Bake at 350º F for 10 minutes. Makes 4 dozen cookies.

Polar Bear Sundae

2 scoops vanilla ice cream
red raspberry dessert sauce
marshmallow crème
wild blueberry syrup

whipped cream
optional garnishes: fresh berries or maraschino cherry, sprig of mint

Using a tulip-shaped glass, pour a small amount of the wild blueberry syrup to the bottom. Place a scoop of ice cream in the glass. Add a dollop of marshmallow crème and another scoop of ice cream. Top with red raspberry, whipped cream and a cherry if desired. A sprig of mint or fresh berries make a nice garnish as well. Makes one sundae.

Polar Bear Drink

1/2 ounce each of crème de cacao and peppermint schnapps

Mix over ice before serving in a shot glass. Tastes like a peppermint patty! For variety, add hot chocolate.

Distinguished Friends of Bears
Paving the Path to Better Human-Bear Relations

Dr. Lynn Rogers

Regarded by many as the Jane Goodall of black bears, Dr. Lynn Rogers is truly one of the great pioneers in his field. He has dedicated his life's work to a better understanding of the true nature of these misunderstood animals.

Rogers has been studying black bears for forty years as a wildlife research biologist. Using airplanes, vehicles, and snowshoes, he has radio-tracked over a hundred bears in the vast forests of northeastern Minnesota, studying some individuals for as long as twenty-two years. Using rather unorthodox research techniques, Rogers learned that he could form trusting relationships with these intelligent animals; even with mothers who had cubs. He began spending 24-hour periods walking and resting with them, detailing their activities, diet, ecology, social organization, vocalizations, and more. Today, he literally lives with his study subjects; black bears are frequent and regular visitors to his research facility. His unique ability to build trusting relationships with his research bears allows him to radio collar them without the use of a tranquilizer.

New discoveries continue to be made as Rogers focuses on learning how we can better coexist with bears. His ongoing work is the source of much of the scientific information on black bears available today. He has written over a hundred scientific articles on black bear behavior and ecology and has edited many scientific articles, books, and TV scripts to assure accuracy before they are published or broadcast. He shares his knowledge through lectures, workshops, and museum exhibits and is a consultant for legislatures, government agencies, and private organizations across America. For over three decades, the media has carried his information to millions of people each year, contributing to an improved public attitude toward black bears.

As a widely published, award-winning photographer, Rogers has captured some incredibly tender and intimate moments few of us have ever had the pleasure to witness firsthand. His photographs have been published in *National Geographic*, *National Wildlife Magazine* and *Field & Stream,* among many others.

Much of his life's work is now proudly on display at the recently opened North American Bear Center in Ely, Minnesota. Here you will have the opportunity to view bears up close and personal in the natural outdoor enclosure. Field study courses, taught by Rogers, are also available through the Wildlife Research Institute *(see page 164–165 for more information).*

www.bear.org • www.bearstudy.org

Dr. Stephen Herrero

The recipient of a number of highly distinguished awards, Dr. Stephen Herrero still considers himself to be "a boring academic, passionately interested in bears, but still mainly a scientist." Nothing could be further from the truth. While he is genuinely modest, he is anything but boring. He is a truly outstanding and fascinating individual who has inspired tremendous caring and passion in his students and colleagues, as well as audiences across the globe. Herrero is one of the most highly respected bear biologists in the business. He has participated in numerous committees and groups aimed at understanding and conserving bears, not the least of which include being past president of the International Association for Bear Research and Management (IBA) and past chair of IUCN Bear Specialist Group.

Although he is recognized throughout the world as a leading authority on bear ecology, behavior, conservation, and management, he is perhaps best known for his research on bear attacks and his book: *Bear Attacks: Their Causes and Avoidance*—over 100,000 copies have been sold, plus it has been translated into German and Japanese. He is a professor emeritus of Environmental Science at the University of Calgary in Canada.

In 1967, when the shaggy-haired Herrero had just finished his graduate work at Berkeley, he and his family piled in their Volkswagen van and headed on vacation, going to visit several of the great national parks. They were on their way to Glacier National Park when the news broke that two women had been killed by grizzlies there, in separate incidents. From that day forward, Herrero became fascinated by bear behavior and ecology. He set out to learn all he could about bear attacks, collecting data about attacks dating back to the days of Lewis and Clark. Today, he is called upon to investigate bear attacks and hired by national parks and other jurisdictions to advise them on how to prevent attacks and keep parks and other natural areas safe.

Herrero continues to make an immense contribution to the body of science on bears, both at home in Canada as well as internationally, from Alaska and Yellowstone to Japan, Mexico and China. His work is dedicated to applying research and knowledge to solving complex, real world, and interdisciplinary problems. He is currently involved in several research projects on bear-human interactions, and also carries out bear and other wildlife safety training and planning.

www.ucalgary.ca/evds/herrero

Benjamin Kilham

A licensed bear rehabilitator, naturalist and author, Benjamin Kilham may be better known as Papa Bear or Mother Bear Man. He raises orphaned black bear cubs in the wild, and in the process he learns as much about their behavior as he can.

The Kilham family had a reputation for taking in wayward wildlife, and in the spring of 1993 he ended up with two severely malnourished bear cubs that only weighed four pounds. His goal was to raise and observe them, and release them back to the wild. He was keen to study young animals so that he could follow them through their life cycle. Getting to know how bears interact with each other and with humans has been the focus of his work. By watching bears grow and respond to their environment, Kilham believed he could gain unique insight into their behavior.

According to Kilham, "Instead of keeping them in a cage, my idea was to walk with and handle them without restraint, and to do so in an unfenced, big-woods setting." But to accomplish this he would have to break tradition and establish a relationship with the cubs, without encouraging dependency. His methods are controversial. All conventional theory indicated that these cubs would become habituated to people in general. As radical as his plan was, he has successfully raised and released two dozen cubs.

Kilham's role as "mother bear" is not so much to teach the bears the ropes, but to provide the safety of a foster parent to protect them against danger while they find their own way in the world.

You can meet many of the fascinating and memorable ursine characters Kilham has raised in his book and videos. Benjamin Kilham's book, *Among the Bears: Raising Orphan Cubs in the Wild,* is a personal story of the bond between animals and humans. In addition to his latest film from National Geographic, *Man Among Bears*, Kilham has appeared in and taken part in the production of several other documentaries. His presentations have entertained thousands of ursophiles, with Kilham's personal and passionate accounts illuminating the intimate lives of bears.

www.BenKilham.com

Carrie Hunt

During her thirty years of research and observation of bear behavior, Carrie Hunt has come to know what makes bears tick and what it takes to turn them away from trouble. She is the founder of the Wind River Bear Institute, a nonprofit organization whose aim is to reduce human-bear conflicts and promote coexistence between bears and people.

Hunt tested the use of pepper spray, rubber bullets, and Karelian Bear Dogs (KBD) to teach bears to avoid people and developed areas. Often, bears that get into trouble with people are trapped and relocated, and if the bear returns, it is killed—not a popular or long-term solution. Hunt and her team of KBD's, however, teach bears in conflict a life-saving lesson. When a bear decides to break the rules and steal a meal from a ranch or campsite, Hunt's ability to face it down and teach it "no" can mean the difference between life and death.

The Karelian bear dogs shepherd bears out of places they should not be, barking ferociously. Hunt and her team provide the backup, shooting rubber bullets at the bears, tossing loud "firecrackers" in their direction, and shouting, "Get out of here, bear!" As soon as the bear runs back into the woods, the team is silent. The idea, according to Hunt, is to punish bears for approaching and reward them for running away—a simple strategy that's proven quite useful.

While it is a tough-love approach, a KBD's bark is far worse than its bite. The dogs never touch a bear; they work as a group on long leashes to intimidate bears by barking so loudly and so relentlessly that it's impossible for the bear to continue its pillaging act.

While the dogs were originally used in Finland and Russia to track and hunt bears, Hunt also uses her Karelians as ambassadors to build bridges with people, teaching them how to stop attracting bears onto their properties in the first place.

Called Partners-In-Life, Hunt's Bear Shepherding Program has been implemented in numerous national parks and towns throughout North America, and as far away as Japan, with amazing results. Hunt has dedicated her life to teaching people how to improve their relationship with bears. Her work has undoubtedly saved the lives of many bruins. Wildlife managers are even trying her techniques on other species of wildlife, such as bighorn sheep and moose.

www.beardogs.org

Charlie Russell

Charlie Russell, a renowned naturalist, writer, and photographer, has spent more than forty years studying bears. As a child growing up in Alberta's grizzly country, he worked with his father Andy *(see page 66)* to learn about grizzly and black bears. Later, as a guide in British Columbia's Khutzeymateen Valley, his knowledge of and appreciation for bears grew steadily. Soon after, Russell found himself working to protect the Kermode bears of Princess Royal Island. There, while working on a film with Jeff and Sue Turner, he became intrigued with and eventually befriended the shy young Spirit bear who was the subject of the film, *Island of the Ghost Bear*. And so began Russell's quest to forge a unique relationship of mutual trust with bears.

From 1997 to 2003, Russell spent the summers living in a remote cabin in the South Kamchatka Sanctuary in Russia, where he raised a trio of brown bears rescued from a zoo. In fact, raising young orphans became a passion for Russell, and he was to become the proud parent of many more cubs over the years. This gave Russell the opportunity to study these awe-inspiring, yet all too frequently misunderstood animals. He carefully observed what would happen if people replaced fear, anger and aggression with openness, kindness, and trust. His findings were remarkable. His current work has brought him full circle back to British Columbia and Alberta, Canada to focus on coexisting with the bears at home.

Through his breathtaking photography and heart-warming stories, Russell helps us understand and celebrate the magnificence of bears. His amazing work has forced people to reconsider an age-old image of the bear as a ferocious man-eater who can't live in harmony with people. Russell has several books to his credit, including *Grizzly Seasons, Grizzly Heart: Living Without Fear Among the Brown Bears of Kamchatka* and *Spirit Bear*; all well worth the read. He has also appeared in many documentaries, including *Bear Man of Kamchatka* (a.k.a. *Edge of Eden: Living with Grizzlies*) and *Walking with Giants: The Grizzlies of Siberia*.

Russell has learned to appreciate the true nature of bears. His unprejudiced understanding and fearless approach allow him to interact with bears at a level of comfort that would send shivers up most anyone's spine. He describes his studies as more sociological than biological. While his theories are at odds with current thinking, he has undoubtedly brought a new dimension to human-bear interactions, based on people developing a respectful, but gentler, wilderness etiquette.

www.cloudline.org

Recommended Resources

BOOKS

Bears: An Altitude SuperGuide
by Kevin Van Tighem; Altitude
Publishing Ltd., 1997

The Bears and I by Robert Franklin
Leslie; Ballantine Books, 1968

**Bear Attacks: Their Causes and
Avoidance (Revised Edition)** by
Stephen Herrero; Lyons Press, 2002

**Bears: Monarchs of the Northern
Wilderness** by Wayne Lynch;
Graystone Books, 1993

**The Black Grizzly of Whiskey
Creek** by Sid Marty; Emblem
Editions, 2008

**Living with Bears: A Practical
Guide to Bear Country** by Linda
Masterson; PixyJack Press, 2006

**The Sacred Paw: The Bear in
Nature, Myth, and Literature** by
Paul Shepard and Barry Sanders;
Penguin, 1992

BOOKS FOR KIDS

Bears, Bears, Bears by Wayne
Lynch; Firefly Books, 1995

Bear Smart Kids by Evelyn Kirkaldy;
Get Bear Smart Society, 2006

Discovering Black Bears by
Margaret Anderson, Nancy Field,
and Karen Stephenson; Dog-Eared
Publications, 2007

FOR TEACHERS

**Wild About Bears! An Educator's
Activity Guide** (for K–7 educators)
Wild BC
www.hctf.ca/wild/resources

ON-LINE DOWNLOADS

**Living with Predators Resource
Guides**
Living With Wildlife Foundation
www.lwwf.org/projects.htm

VIDEOS

**Staying Safe in Bear County
Living in Bear Country**
Wild Eye Productions
www.distributionaccess.com

**Bear With Me: A Young Person's
Guide to Black Bear Safety**
Pinegrove Productions
For home use, contact
pinegrove@superaje.com
For educational distribution:
McNabb Connolly
www.mcnabbconnolly.ca

WEB SITES

**Alaska Department of Fish &
Game Wildlife Conservation**
www.wildlife.alaska.gov

**The American Bear Association:
Vince Shute Wildlife Sanctuary**
www.americanbear.org

CONTINUED...

Animals Asia Foundation
www.animalsasia.org

Get Bear Smart Society
www.bearsmart.com

Great Bear Foundation
www.greatbear.org

Grizzly Bay
www.grizzlybay.org

The Humane Society of the United States
www.hsus.org

International Association for Bear Research and Management (IBA)
www.bearbiology.org

Living with Wildlife Foundation
www.lwwf.org

MotherNature.com: A Guide to Living and Playing Safely in Bear Country
www.mountainnature.com/Wildlife/Bears/

National Park Service
www.nps.gov
    Katmai National Park & Preserve
    www.nps.gov/katm

North American Bear Center
www.bear.org

Ontario Ministry of Natural Resources: Bear Wise
www.mnr.gov.on.ca/en/Business/Bearwise

Polar Bears International
www.polarbearsinternational.org

Valhalla Wilderness Society
www.vws.org

Vital Ground
www.vitalground.org

Whistler Blackcomb: Bear Viewing and Ecology Tours
www.whistlerblackcomb.com/todo/summer/bears

Wildlife Research Institute
www.bearstudy.org

WildWatch
www.bear-viewing-in-alaska.info

Wind River Bear Institute
www.beardogs.org

World Society for the Protection of Animals
www.wspa.ca (look for Bear Safe under WSPAs Work / Wildlife)

Zoocheck Canada
www.zoocheck.com

For more information about programs in your own area:
www.BearSmart.com
Select *Backyard Bears - Who Do I Call?* for a list of
bear aware / bear smart / bear wise groups across North America.

ACKNOWLEDGMENTS

While there are many people who have contributed to my knowledge of and passion for bears, my husband Steve is my most loyal supporter. Thank you with all my heart for accompanying me on my journey into the world of the bear.

I am indebted to Evelyn Kirkaldy for her artistic support. She has not only provided the fabulous illustrations in this book, she also draws all of the illustrations used in the Get Bear Smart Society's educational materials, portraying bears in an honest and accurate style.

Heartfelt thanks to Jeff Gailus and Lori Homstol for their ongoing support, dedication and written contributions. Many thanks, too, to Irene Sheppard and all the photographers who so generously contributed their work. A truckload of gratitude to David Krughoff, in particular, for his photographs and his expertise in the digital darkroom.

I am grateful to those whose websites and books were a great resource for information, ideas and trivia: Jessica and John Teel; Vince Shute Wildlife Sanctuary (VSWS), American Bear Center and Wildlife Research Institute (WRI); Margaret Anderson, Nancy Field and Karen Stephenson; R. W. Sandford; and many others too numerous to mention.

I would not have been able to write this book without the courage and wisdom of Dr. Lynn Rogers. I have learned more about bears by spending time with him at WRI than from any book I will ever read. Many thanks also to Klari Lea and VSWS—the largest open-air classroom in North America to learn about black bears—where I have spent many happy and memorable times taking photographs and video.

Thanks to my wonderful Board of Directors: Ainslie Willock, Crystal McMillan, Wayne McCrory, Dan LeGrandeur and Dr. John Beecham. Without their expertise, support and guidance, the Get Bear Smart Society would not be the well-respected organization it is today. I also owe much to our team of scientific advisors—Dr. Rogers, Ben Kilham and Carrie Hunt—who provide invaluable input into our Bear Smart initiatives.

A special word of thanks to the Community Foundation of Whistler for supporting the Get Bear Smart Society financially over the years and for providing the seed money to get this book off the ground.

And lastly, a big, big thank you to the bears who bring me so much joy, and who have given me the gift of enthusiasm and passion for my work.

ABOUT THE AUTHOR

Sylvia Dolson's passion for bears is equaled only by her quest to teach people about the true nature of these wonderful bruins. Her ultimate goal is for a greater coexistence—one in which people and bears live in harmony. As a naturalist, wildlife photographer and freelance writer, Sylvia chooses to spend much of her free time in the company of bears. Having walked among wild black bears, polar bears and grizzlies, she has gained an ever-increasing appreciation and understanding of all the wilderness and its inhabitants.

Sylvia has been involved with the Get Bear Smart Society since 1996 and is now the executive director. She is also a member of the International Association for Bear Research and Management. As a leading expert on living with bears in residential communities, she has been instrumental in bringing forward more progressive, bear-friendly management policies in British Columbia, Canada. She currently co-chairs the Whistler Bear Working Group and was the key catalyst and contributor for Whistler's Black Bear Management

Author Sylvia Dolson. *PHOTO: IRENE SHEPPARD*

Plan. Her persistent hard work and dedication have resulted in establishing Whistler as British Columbia's leading Bear Smart community, becoming a model for others to follow.

Sylvia travels throughout North America speaking at conferences and workshops. She has authored many reference materials for educational purposes, maintains an extensive website, and writes a regular newspaper column.

Sylvia and her husband, Steve, live in Whistler, British Columbia, where they share their lives with two canine companions, Samantha and Brandy.

To reach Sylvia Dolson, please email *info@bearsmart.com*.

THE ILLUSTRATOR
EVELYN KIRKALDY

An avid hiker and outdoor enthusiast, Evelyn Kirkaldy's favorite pastime is exploring wild places. She has explored the west coast of British Columbia, traveled to Alaska, and to locations such as Churchill, Manitoba, seeking out bears: black, brown and white. Evelyn is an accomplished artist as well as an educator and dedicated bear advocate. "My artwork is another vehicle with which I am hoping to foster a better understanding of bears." Her artwork can also be seen at *http://flickr.com/photos/evelynkirkaldy*.

GET BEAR SMART SOCIETY

The Get Bear Smart Society (GBS), based in Whistler, British Columbia, Canada, champions progressive management policies that reduce both the number of human-bear conflicts and the number of bears destroyed. Our mission is to provide a safe environment in which people and bears can coexist in harmony. We accomplish this by implementing effective waste management systems, educating people on dealing with bears in their communities as well as minimizing backyard attractants, and promoting innovative, non-lethal bear management practices.

www.bearsmart.com is the most popular resource for information on living with bears, recreating in bear country, and learning about bear biology and ecology. The site also contains information for policy makers and bear aware groups on creating bear-smart communities and offers innovative, non-lethal bear management techniques for bear managers.

Please consider making a donation to help support bear-smart initiatives.

Get Bear Smart Society
P.O. Box 502, Whistler, BC V0N 1B0 Canada
www.bearsmart.com
Email: *info@bearsmart.com*

Check out these Bear Smart products at www.bearsmart.com/store

Wholesale prices are available for stores and bear aware groups.

Playing Cards

Play your way through bear country as you learn to live with your ursine neighbours with Get Bear Smart Playing Cards:

52 Tips on Staying Safe in Bear Country

A Bruin Trivia Game
Designed for kids, but fun for the whole family.

Bumper Stickers

Choose from a variety of weather-resistant vinyl bumper stickers.